How to Excel During Depositions:
Techniques for Experts That Work

STEVEN BABITSKY, ESQ.

JAMES J. MANGRAVITI, Jr., ESQ.

S•E•A•K, Inc.
Legal and Medical Information Systems

Falmouth, Massachusetts

How to Excel During Depositions:
Techniques for Experts That Work

Copyright © 1999 by SEAK, Inc.
Third impression 2003
ISBN: 1-892904-00-4

CONTENTS

Preface

This work has been created as a companion to our 1997 text, *How to Excel During Cross-Examination: Techniques for Experts That Work.* It has been designed to empower experts from all fields to excel at deposition—the format (as opposed to appearing in court at trial) that sees the vast majority of expert testimony. As in our *Cross-Examination* work, we have attempted to teach by example. As such, this work contains over 150 examples of question and answer exchanges from depositions. Most of this material is taken verbatim from actual expert deposition testimony in real cases. Each example contains a "lesson" in which we explain some of the more important points that can be learned and should be remembered from the example.

We have designed the book to be easy and fun to read. The detailed index and table of contents have been designed to make it a more valuable bookshelf reference. We sincerely hope you find *How to Excel During Depositions: Techniques for Experts That Work* to be a valuable resource and we welcome your feedback on this work.

Steven Babitsky, Esq.
James J. Mangraviti, Jr., Esq.
SEAK, Inc.
PO Box 729
Falmouth, MA 02541

Acknowledgments

The authors wish to acknowledge the following persons whose assistance in the production of this book was invaluable: Ronald S. Beitman, Esq.; John C. Cabaniss, Esq.; Robert B. Fredericks, Esq.; Ronald D. Glotta, Esq.; Kenneth I. Kolpan, Esq.; Richard K. Latimer, Esq.; David M. Lawson, Esq.; Philip F. Mulvey, Jr., Esq.; Alan Pierce, Esq.; Barry C. Reed, Jr., Esq.; David R. Schmidt, Esq.; Geoff Shapiro, Esq.; Bruce H. Stern, Esq.; and Christopher J. Todd, JD. The authors would also like to acknowledge the invaluable input of Kathy Lamson and Dee Netzel for their assistance in the production and editing of this book.

Related Products by SEAK, Inc.

<u>TEXTS</u>
The Independent Medical Examination Report:
A Step-by-Step Guide with Models

How to Excel During Cross-Examination:
Techniques for Experts That Work

The Comprehensive IME System: Essential Resources
for an Efficient and Successful IME Practice

The Successful Physician Negotiator: How to Get What
You Deserve

<u>SEMINARS</u>
SEAK Law School for Physicians ™

How to Be an Effective Medical Witness

How to Be a Successful Independent Medical Examiner

SEAK Negotiating Skills for Physicians ™

SEAK Business School for Physicians ™

National Expert Witness and Litigation Seminar

<u>AUDIOTAPE PROGRAMS</u>
Achieving Success as a Medical Witness

For more information call SEAK at 508/457-1111.
Inquiries may also be addressed to SEAK, Inc. at
P.O. Box 729, Falmouth, MA 02541. Fax 508/540-
8304; e-mail address: seakinc@aol.com; Internet
address: http://www.seak.com

About the Authors

Steven Babitsky, Esq., is the president of SEAK, Inc. He was a personal injury trial attorney for 20 years and is the former managing partner of the firm Kistin, Babitsky, Latimer & Beitman. He is the editor of *The Expert Witness Journal* and the seminar leader for the National Expert Witness and Litigation Seminar. Attorney Babitsky is the co-author of the text *How to Excel During Cross-Examination: Techniques for Experts that Work.* Attorney Babitsky is the co-developer and trainer for the "How to Be an Effective Medical Witness" seminar and the scriptwriter for the video *How to Be an Effective Medical Witness.*

James J. Mangraviti, Jr., Esq., is a former trial lawyer with experience in defense and plaintiff personal injury law and insurance law. He currently serves as vice-president and general counsel of SEAK, Inc. Mr. Mangraviti received his B.A. degree in mathematics *summa cum laude* from Boston College and his J.D. degree *cum laude* from Boston College Law School. His publications include the texts *The Independent Medical Examination Report: A Step-by-Step Guide with Models, How to Excel During Cross-Examination: Techniques for Experts that Work,* and *The Successful Physician Negotiator: How to Get What You Deserve.* Mr. Mangraviti has trained hundreds of expert witnesses across the United States and Canada.

Chapter 1 Deposition Law and Procedure

1.1 What Is an Expert Deposition?

A deposition is defined as

> the testimony of a witness taken upon oral question
> or written interrogatories, not in open court, but in
> pursuance of a commission to take testimony issued
> by a court, or under a general law or court rule on
> the subject, and reduced to writing and duly
> authenticated, and intended to be used in preparation
> and upon the trial of a civil action or criminal
> prosecution.[1]

An expert deposition is the deposition of a person who
has been designated as an *expert witness* in a case.
Expert witnesses are witnesses who, due to their
"knowledge, skill, experience, training, or education,"[2]
may give testimony in the form of an opinion. An
expert witness needs to be contrasted with a *fact
witness*. Generally, a fact witness's testimony is limited
to what the witness observed, heard, smelled, tasted, or
felt. Fact witnesses generally are not allowed to testify
in the form of an opinion.

    The witness whose deposition is being taken or
who is being deposed is called the *deponent*. The
deponent's testimony during a deposition is made under
oath under the pains and penalties of perjury.
Generally, depositions may be taken by means of

---

[1] Henry Campbell Black, *Black's Law Dictionary, Sixth Edition*
(St. Paul, MN: West Publishing Co., 1990) 440.
[2] Federal Rule of Evidence 702.

written questions propounded to the deponent.[3] In practice, this form of deposition is utilized only very rarely because it does not allow for the all-important follow-up questions to an evasive or noncooperative deponent.

Example 1.1

Q: But specifically, Doctor, have you been asked to take an individual worker or a group of workers at Ford Motor Company who have carpal tunnel syndrome and tell Ford or the UAW what caused their carpal tunnel?

A: That would be more of a—I specifically look at the jobs. And some of those people have been diagnosed with carpal tunnel.

Q: But were you asked by Ford and the UAW to tell them what caused their carpal tunnel?

A: What caused it? Well, I think the known cause is the work but I identified the specific aspects of the job.

Q: You went in and identified the workplace for risk factors and said here's how to correct it, correct?

A: We know that carpal tunnel is caused by the work. They don't ask that question. It's not an issue.

Q: So, you weren't asked to do that, correct?

A: No. They don't ask that 'cause they know the jobs, that type of work can cause carpal tunnel.

Lesson: Responses to questions can be evasive or non-responsive. The oral deposition allows the questioner to follow up with questions. It is therefore much more effective for gathering information than are submitted written questions.

---

[3] See Federal Rule of Civil Procedure 31 which states in part, "A party may take the testimony of any person, including a party, by deposition upon written questions without leave of court...."

Depositions in civil cases are engendered and governed by the rules of civil procedure of the court where the action is pending. These rules will vary from state to state. For example, the rules of civil procedure governing a civil action filed in a Massachusetts state court are not the same as the rules that would govern a civil action filed in a New York state court. The Federal Rules of Civil Procedure govern actions filed in federal court in all fifty states. The Federal Rules have an influence on many of the state rules and will be the basis for many of the discussions in this work.

Depositions are recorded in one or more ways. Normally, a written transcript is prepared by a stenographer who records what is said "on the record" at the deposition. It is also common for those present to have "off the record" discussions during a deposition that are not reflected in the transcript. Deponents should *always* assume, however, that whatever they say at a deposition is being recorded *on* the record.

Depositions may also be videotaped. Videotaped depositions are especially useful to an attorney if the attorney plans on submitting the deposition testimony at trial in lieu of the deponent's live testimony. Expert depositions are frequently videotaped. Presenting expert testimony at trial by way of a videotaped deposition is more economical because the parties do not have to pay for the expert's time to testify at trial. Videotaped depositions may also be used when the attorney is concerned that the witness will not be available for trial because of terminal illness, upcoming travel plans, or other reasons.

1.2 Discovery

Under the Federal Rules of Civil Procedure, a party is allowed various methods of *discovery*. These discovery methods are designed to obtain facts and information about the case from the other parties, persons, or entities. **A deposition is merely one of the procedural methods available under the rules of civil procedure as part of discovery.** Other methods of discovery include written interrogatories, production of documents or things, permission to enter upon land or other property, physical and mental examination, and requests for admissions.

The Federal Rules of Civil Procedure (FRCP) permit very liberal and broad-based discovery. There are two rationales for the liberal discovery procedures that dominate today's civil lawsuits: eliminating surprise at trial and encouraging settlement. The theory is that if all parties know all there is to know about the other side's case, they will be able to evaluate the merits and weaknesses of the case rationally and settle the matter. Additionally, if the suit does go to trial, the outcome will be less dependent upon gamesmanship because the possibility of unfair surprises has been minimized through the liberal discovery process. *An understanding of these two rationales is absolutely essential for any expert who wants to understand his or her role in a civil litigation deposition. These two rationales are the reasons why attorneys are allowed to ask broad, ranging, and pointed questions at deposition.*

To effectuate the goals stated above, the rules provide for *very broad-based* discovery. The scope of discovery is defined in Fed. R. Civ. Pro. 26(b)(1).

> **Fed. R. Civ. Pro. 26(b)(1)**
> Parties may obtain discovery regarding any matter, not privileged, which is relevant to the subject matter involved in the pending action, whether it relates to the claim or defense of the party seeking discovery or to the claim or defense of any other party, including the existence, description, nature, custody, condition, and location of any books, documents, or other tangible things and the identity and location of any persons having knowledge of any discoverable matter. The information sought need not be admissible at trial if the information sought appears reasonably calculated to lead to the discovery of admissible evidence.

1.3 Limits to Discovery

PRIVILEGE

Although discovery is broad-based, it is not unlimited. Privileged information is generally not discoverable.[4] For example, unless the privilege was waived or an exception applies, a privilege may protect information known to a physician about that physician's patient due to the physician-patient privilege. Other commonly asserted privileges include the husband-wife privilege and the attorney-client privilege. The existence and precise scope of the various privileges varies from state to state. If a valid privilege exists, then the expert deponent may refuse to answer questions that would violate that privilege.

Federal Rule 26(b)(2) provides further limits on discovery. As you can see, this rule protects parties from discovery that is overly burdensome or expensive.

---

[4] Fed. R. Civ. Pro. 26(b)(1).

> **Fed. R. Civ. Pro. 26(b)(2)**
> The frequency or extent of use of the discovery methods otherwise permitted under these rules and by any local rule shall be limited by the court if it determines that: (i) the discovery sought is unreasonably cumulative or duplicative, or it is obtainable through some other source that is more convenient, less burdensome, or less expensive; (ii) the party seeking discovery has had ample opportunity by discovery in the action to obtain the information sought; or (iii) the burden or expense of the proposed discovery outweighs its likely benefit, taking into account the needs of the case, the amount in controversy, the parties' resources, the importance of the issues at stake in the litigation, and the importance of the proposed discovery in resolving the issues.

WORK PRODUCT—TRIAL PREPARATION

In addition to privileged material, attorney *work product* is usually nondiscoverable. This exception to liberal discovery is designed to allow the adversary process to function properly. The work product exception to discovery as it applies to expert witnesses is governed by Federal Rule 26(b)(4). This rule, with some exceptions, protects experts who are not to be called as witnesses at trial from being subject to discovery. *Thus, if you are an expert who is working as a consultant and the party retaining you does not intend to call you as a witness at trial, Federal Rule 26(b)(4) will in most cases protect you from ever having to give a deposition in the case.*

Fed. R. Civ. Pro. 26(b)(4) Trial Preparation: Experts

(A) A party may depose any person who has been identified as an expert whose opinions may be presented at trial. If a report from the expert is required under subdivision (a)(2)(B), the deposition shall not be conducted until after the report is provided.

(B) A party may, through interrogatories or by deposition, discover facts known or opinions held by an expert who has been retained or specially employed by another party in anticipation of litigation or preparation for trial and who is not expected to be called as a witness at trial, only as provided in Rule 35(b) or upon a showing of exceptional circumstances under which it is impracticable for the party seeking discovery to obtain facts or opinions on the same subject by other means.

(C) Unless manifest injustice would result, (i) the court shall require that the party seeking discovery pay the expert a reasonable fee for time spent in responding to discovery under this subdivision; and (ii) with respect to discovery obtained under subdivision (b)(4)(B) of this rule the court shall require the party seeking discovery to pay the other party a fair portion of the fees and expenses reasonably incurred by the latter party in obtaining facts and opinions from the expert.

PROTECTIVE ORDERS

The court has discretion to issue *protective orders* to protect a party or person from "annoyance, embarrassment, oppression or undue burden or expense."[5] The court can also issue protective orders to protect "a trade secret, or other confidential research, development or commercial information."[6] Protective orders are issued after a motion is made by the person or party seeking the order. A person need not be a party to the lawsuit to seek a protective order. The granting of a protective order is within the court's sound discretion. When granting a protective order, the court may rule that the discovery be limited or disallowed, rule that the discovery only be made available to certain persons, or limit the method of discovery utilized.[7] Protective orders relevant to expert depositions include a request by an attorney to reduce what he or she considers to be an unreasonable fee from an expert witness or a request by an expert to prevent discovery of personal and sensitive information.

SANCTIONS

If a party, deponent, or attorney unjustifiably refuses to disclose requested information, the party seeking the information can make a *motion to compel* the party or deponent to provide the requested discovery. This motion is made to the court (the judge). If the motion to compel is granted, the party seeking the discovery may also seek sanctions against the party, deponent, and/or attorney refusing to provide the discovery.[8] The potential sanctions include the costs of bringing the motion to compel, including attorney's fees. If the motion to compel is *denied*, the party and/or attorney

---

[5] Fed. R. Civ. Pro. 26(c).
[6] Fed. R. Civ. Pro. 26(c)(7).
[7] Fed. R. Civ. Pro. 26(c).
[8] See, e.g., *Nationwide Mutual Fire Insurance Company v. Smith*, 174 F.R.D. 250 (D.Conn. 1997) and *Hearst/ABC-Viacom Entertainment Services v. Goodway Marketing, Inc.*, 145 F.R.D. 59 E.D. Pa. 1992).

bringing the motion to compel may be ordered by the court to pay the attorney's fees and costs of the person or party from whom discovery is sought. For example, if you refused to answer certain questions during your expert deposition, counsel could file a motion to compel to have the court order that you answer the propounded questions. If this motion is granted, counsel can then move for sanctions against you. If counsel's motion to compel is denied, you could move for sanctions against the attorney.

1.4 Stipulations, Objections, and Instructions Not to Answer

STIPULATIONS

A *stipulation* is an agreement between counsel regarding facts or procedure. In many jurisdictions counsel will start the deposition and agree to the "usual" or "standard" stipulations.

Example 1.2
Counsel: We'll have the doctor read and sign. Otherwise, usual stipulations?
Counsel: Yes.

Lesson: It is important for you to understand what these "usual" or "standard" stipulations are and mean.

Frequently, these stipulations are spelled out by counsel for the record. For example:

It is hereby stipulated and agreed by and between counsel for the respective parties that the witness shall read and sign the deposition transcript within

30 days of receipt of said transcript, otherwise, it
shall be deemed to have been waived and the
notarization of the witness's signature is waived. It
is further stipulated and agreed that all objections,
except as to form, and motions to strike are reserved
until the time of trial.

What this stipulation means is that the lawyers
are agreeing that they won't make any objections to
questions except as to the form of the question. Under
this agreement, counsel could object if he or she felt the
question was compound, leading, or confusing, but
would reserve objections with other evidentiary bases
such as relevancy, unfair prejudice, and hearsay until
trial. A frequent complaint by experts is that "the
attorney just sat there, silent," while the other attorney
questioned the expert closely. Often, the reason why
attorneys don't object during depositions is that under
the standard stipulations, the only proper objections are
to the form of the question.
State and local rules and customs may vary from
jurisdiction to jurisdiction, thus the expert should
acquaint herself with the local rules and customs or
stipulations at deposition. Note that in the standard
stipulation the expert witness has 30 days within which
to read and sign the deposition transcript. During this
30-day period, the expert can correct any errors in the
deposition transcript. If you are not clear about the
stipulations or do not agree with them, you must speak
up immediately to preserve your rights. Consider the
following example.

Example 1.3
Counsel A: Stipulations?
Counsel B: She would like to waive the reading and
signing.

Expert: I would like to read and sign the deposition, sir.

Counsel B: Sorry. The witness reserves the right to read and sign the deposition transcript within 30 days of receipt of said transcript.

Lesson: You generally have a right to read and sign your deposition.[9] You shouldn't let counsel waive that right unless you want to.

OBJECTIONS

The general rule regarding objections by counsel at deposition is contained in Rule 30 of the Federal Rules of Civil Procedure.

> **Fed. R. Civ. Pro. 30(d) Schedule and Duration; Motion to Terminate or Limit Examination.**
> (1) Any objection to evidence during a deposition shall be stated concisely and in a non-argumentative and non-suggestive manner. A party may instruct a deponent not to answer only when necessary to preserve a privilege, to enforce a limitation on evidence directed by the court, or to present a motion under paragraph (3).

FRCP 32 provides further insight into what objections can and should be made at deposition by counsel. As you can see, in many cases the rules do not require the attorneys to make certain objections at deposition.

---

[9] Under the Federal Rules of Civil Procedure, this right to read and sign is not self-executing. The party or deponent must *request* reading and signing prior to the completion of the deposition. (See Fed. R. Civ. Pro. 30(e).)

> **Fed. R. Civ. Pro. 32 Use of Depositions in Court Proceedings**
>
> (b) Objections to Admissibility. Subject to the provisions of Rule 28(b) and subdivision (d)(3) of this rule, objection may be made at the trial or hearing to receiving in evidence any deposition or part thereof for any reason which would require the exclusion of the evidence if the witness were then present and testifying....
>
> (d)(3)(B) Effect of Errors and Irregularities in Depositions. Errors and irregularities occurring at the oral examination in the manner of taking the deposition, in the form of the questions or answers, in the oath or affirmation, or in the conduct of parties, and errors of any kind which might be obviated, removed, or cured if promptly presented, are waived unless reasonable objection thereto is made at the taking of the deposition.

What this means as a practical matter is that the standard objections covered by counsel may include:

- form of the question (e.g., leading the witness),
- competency,
- relevancy,
- materiality, and
- nonresponsive answer.

If a stipulation of counsel reserves all objections except those regarding form until the time of the trial, counsel will just state, "Objection." In other cases, counsel will spell out his or her objection on the record.

Requiring the specific grounds for objections permits counsel propounding the question to cure or correct the question so that it is no longer objectionable.

You should listen carefully to the objection because it may reveal some tips or insight into the questioning.

Your role as an expert is not to argue evidence or procedure. You are *not* an advocate and will lose credibility if you appear to be one. With this in mind, the authors recommend that experts do the following when an objection is made.

1. Stop testifying immediately.
2. Listen carefully to the objection.
3. Learn as much as you can about the grounds for the objection.
4. Let the lawyers battle it out between themselves.
5. Resume testifying when counsel so instructs you.

Example 1.4
Counsel A: Objection. That answer was totally non-responsive. Move to strike the entire answer.
Counsel B: Let me ask the question another way. Do you have any advanced training in mechanical engineering?
Expert: Yes, I do.
Counsel B: What training did you receive?

Lesson: By listening to the objection, the expert is aware of what the attorney found objectionable (the nonresponsive nature of the answer).

Some counsel use *speaking objections* to coach, tip off, or suggest answers to experts who are being deposed. While this practice is improper[10] and can result in sharp rebukes to counsel, it is not uncommon. You should, therefore, listen very carefully to the objections of counsel.

Example 1.5
Q: Your testimony was, "So we have to establish exactly under what conditions it is possible." Do you recall saying that?
A: I don't recall those words, no.
      Counsel: What was the reference for...?
Q: 181 lines 12 through 16.
      Counsel: I have an objection. It's out of context.
A: I was just going to say it's out of context. I can't comment on it.

Q: My question is: Accepting as true that he is of the opinion or he did a study in which he showed where patients with a Glasgow Coma Scale of 15 in the emergency room, he has documented, have had long-term traumatic brain injury.
      Counsel: I object to the form of the question. I don't think it's fair to the witness to even ask a question like that without giving him the opportunity to know more about what the Reiten study is, who was studied, why they were studied, and whether there was traumatic injury or whether it was stroke, or whatever.
A: I really need to know more about the study before I answer that question accurately.

---

[10] The Federal Rules of Civil Procedure require that objections be stated in a "non-suggestive manner." (See Fed. R. Civ. Pro. 30(d)(1).)

Lesson: The experts in the above cases may have carefully listened to the objections. This may have helped them to organize their thoughts in preparation for truthful, nonobjectionable answers.

INSTRUCTIONS NOT TO ANSWER

You may be instructed not to answer by the counsel who retained you. Under the Federal Rules, an attorney may only instruct a deponent not to answer to preserve a privilege, to enforce a limitation of evidence directed by the court, or to present a motion that the deposition is being "conducted in bad faith or in such a manner as unreasonably to annoy, embarrass, or oppress."[11] Ultimately, the legitimacy of any instruction not to answer may be evaluated by the court. Under the Federal Rules, the deponent or party may be forced to pay the other party's attorney's fees involved in bringing a motion to compel an answer if the instruction not to answer was not substantially justified.[12] If the motion to compel asking the court to order that the deponent answer the question fails and was not substantially justified, the expert and party may file a motion to collect their attorney's fees associated with the filing of the motion to compel.[13] For example, attorney's fees were awarded after improper instructions not to answer were issued in the cases *Nationwide Mutual Fire Insurance Company v. Smith*, 174 F.R.D. 250 (D.Conn. 1997), and *Hearst/ABC-Viacom Entertainment Services v. Goodway Marketing, Inc.*, 145 F.R.D. 59 (E.D. Pa. 1992).

---

[11] Fed. R. Civ. Pro. 30(d).
[12] Fed. R. Civ. Pro. 37(a)(4).
[13] Fed. R. Civ. Pro. 37(a)(4).

Example 1.6

Q: And it's your testimony that you did not intentionally give false testimony to the jury in that trial?

A: That's correct. May I consult with counsel?

Q: No.

A: I need a break, sir.... After break....

> **Counsel:** I am going to object to the question as being asked in bad faith with the intention of embarrassing the witness.... I am instructing the witness not to answer the question.

Q: Counsel, if you are asserting a privilege, please state it for the record. If not, the witness is to answer the question.

Lesson: Instructions not to answer are only proper under limited circumstances. Misuse of the instruction not to answer may result in the deponent and/or the attorney paying the opposing side's attorney's fees associated with bringing a motion to compel.

Chapter 2 Why Experts Are Deposed

The deposing attorney's goals in an expert deposition will vary depending upon why he or she is taking the deposition. The attorney's objectives will vary depending upon which attorney is calling you to testify and whether the deposition is for discovery purposes or to preserve your testimony to be used at trial in lieu of your live appearance.

2.1 Preservation of Evidence Depositions

If you are being deposed by the counsel that retained you, this is most likely done in an effort to preserve your testimony for trial. The attorney that retained you is taking your deposition because either: a) he or she is concerned that you will not be available to testify at trial due to death, disability, or travel or, b) he or she does not want to pay you to appear live at trial and testify. When the retaining party notices your deposition, he or she is most likely planning on either reading the deposition transcript to the jury at trial or showing the jury the videotape of your deposition. Videotape depositions are discussed in much greater detail in Chapter 8.

2.2 Discovery Depositions

When you are deposed by the opposing side and are expected to testify live at trial, this is known as a discovery deposition. As you will recall from Chapter 1, the goals of the discovery process are to allow the attorneys on each side to find out as much as possible (subject to the limits specified in the applicable Rules of Civil Procedure) about the other side's case. The Rules allow this discovery in an attempt to encourage settlement by "putting each party's cards on the table" and to lock in each witness's testimony so as to avoid surprises at trial.

Generally speaking, counsel deposing you during a discovery deposition will attempt to achieve ten major goals.

GOAL 1: YOUR OPINIONS

Counsel wants to learn and clarify your opinion, the basis for your opinion, how the opinion was formed (i.e., the methodology used), when you arrived at the opinion, what future tests and evaluations you are planning, and whether you are willing to modify or change the opinion. Your opinion is the only reason you are allowed to testify as an expert witness. Determining the exact nature, extent, and basis of your opinion is critical for the opposing attorney as he seeks to both prepare for trial and to evaluate the settlement value of the case.

Example 2.1
Q: Doctor, is the opinion that you've expressed here today etched in stone?
A: Etched in stone? Would you want to define that?
Q: Are you willing to change your opinion?
A: Am I willing to change it? I still don't grasp what you're getting at.
Q: Is your opinion inflexible?
A: I don't think my opinion is inflexible.
Q: So you're willing to consider other information and change the opinion that you've stated here today?
A: I would be if the information convinced me otherwise. (See pages 79-82 on opinions.)

Lesson: The fact that you may be willing to change your opinion if you are presented with new facts is important. Counsel may follow up this line of questioning by presenting just that—new and different facts.

GOAL 2: QUALIFICATIONS

Opposing counsel wants to learn as much as possible about your qualifications. Specifically, you may be questioned about your background, education, training, and experience. Counsel may question you thoroughly about your CV. Of particular importance is your experience with situations matching, or closely resembling, the current situation. Juries sometimes find experience, or lack thereof, to be the most relevant factor in weighing your qualifications to give an opinion in a case. The information obtained during the expert deposition can be used at cross-examination during trial in an effort to lessen your credibility. The strengths and weaknesses of your qualifications are also important points of discussion between counsel during settlement negotiations.

Example 2.2
Q: Mr. Breen, I'm going to hand you what has been provided to me and represented to be your current curriculum vitae. Is that in fact the most recent CV that you have?
A: I think so.
Q: Now, you graduated from the University of Illinois in metallurgy in 1978, is that correct?
A: The Department of Materials Engineering.
Q: When you were going to school at the University of Illinois, did you refer to yourself as a metallurgist?
A: No, I didn't.

Q: In your education did you take any courses that would fall into the realm of engineering mechanics other than introductory-level statics and dynamics?
A: Yes.
Q: What courses?
A: I don't recall them, the courses. I took courses in machine design, a course in design called maybe Strength of Members or something like that.
Q: And it's your testimony that the courses you took that involved strength of members were classified as engineering mechanics courses?
A: I don't recall what they classified them as!

Lesson: Counsel is attempting to establish a lack of a proper and relevant educational background, which may be relevant to the witness's qualifications to proffer an opinion in the case. Thus, the witness should carefully consider his answers. If counsel can get his hands on the witness's college transcripts (for example, as part of a licensing application that is public record) he will have precise evidence as to which courses the witness did and did not take.

GOAL 3: LOCK DOWN THE EXPERT

An all-important goal of counsel during a discovery deposition is to lock in your testimony. When you are deposed you are giving testimony under oath. Your testimony is recorded by a stenographer. Once you give an answer to a question at a deposition it can be very problematic to give a different answer to the same question at trial. If you do, the cross-examining attorney can bring into evidence the inconsistent answer that you gave at the deposition. This process of using your prior inconsistent deposition testimony during cross-examination at trial is called *impeachment*. Impeachment can have a severe adverse effect on a witness's credibility at trial. Locking down your testimony so that you can be impeached if you contradict it at trial is a primary goal of counsel.

Example 2.3

Q: If you're asked at trial in this case, "Was Celena Navarro negligent in not riding with direct supervision?" are you going to give an answer?
A: Yes.
Q: And what's your opinion?
A: I believe she was.

Lesson: The expert is now locked into her opinion regarding supervision. If she changes this opinion at trial, she will be confronted with and impeached by her prior inconsistent statement at deposition.

Example 2.4

Q: Are you going to be postulating at trial an opinion that this child's cerebral palsy was caused by an infection?
A: I hope not.
Q: Are you going to be offering any opinion with respect to what caused this child's cerebral palsy?
A: I believe I'd like to be able to offer an opinion of what I conclude appeared to be going on in the delivery room related to the child, which might then have an implication for the status of the child at the time of delivery.

Lesson: If the expert witness later testifies at trial that he believed the cerebral palsy was caused by an infection, he can be confronted with and impeached by his prior statement on this point at deposition.

Example 2.5

Q: So the most significant lab value which one would need to know, the most significant laboratory test or blood test to take to establish metabolic acidosis at the time of delivery is taking an umbilical artery blood sample; is that fair to say?

A: I think that's fair.

Lesson: The expert's deposition testimony will be used to impeach him at trial if he attempts to change his answer on this issue.

GOAL 4: EVALUATE THE PROBABLE CREDIBILITY OF THE DEPONENT IN FRONT OF A JURY

All trials come down to one issue and one issue only—credibility. A major goal of counsel at deposition is to determine the likely credibility of a witness when the witness will appear at trial in front of the jury. Counsel wants to determine if the jury is likely to be sympathetic to and will be likely to believe the expert. Factors such as demeanor and communications skills are important in this analysis. Is the expert attractive and well groomed? Does he or she communicate well or does the expert speak with an accent or talk over people? Is the expert arrogant or evasive? How does this person respond to surprise questions? Is the expert prepared and well organized? Does he or she speak loud enough that the jury will be able to hear? Even innocent sounding "jokes" or flip remarks by an expert during deposition may give counsel insight into how an expert's testimony will appear to the jury or fact finder. How an expert will play in front of a jury is crucial for determining cross-examination strategy and for evaluating the settlement value of the case. It is also crucial in determining how valuable a certain expert is.

Example 2.6

Q: What is aggravation to a medical professional or to an orthopedic surgeon?

A: Something that an attorney does to a doctor.

Q: Let me ask you this. What role, if any, did Honda's dealers play in communicating ATV-related safety information to users back in the 1980-1985 time frame?

A: That's one of these, How would I know?

Q: If you don't, you don't know.

A: I don't know.

Q: The next packet, I assume, sir, you looked at since it's the test results and it's six pages long.

A: I'll plead the Fifth.

Lesson: Expert witnesses are well advised to avoid flip, clever, or joking remarks. Such remarks lessen your credibility as a witness and will accordingly lessen your value to the attorneys that retain you.

Example 2.7

Q: We are at the offices of Equitable Management Associates, Inc.?

A: That's correct.

Q: Sir, I saw the sign on the door on the way in and I didn't see your name on it.

A: It's not—it's a group practice. My name will be put on the directory very soon.

Q: Okay. Maybe you can answer something, a mystery that I have, and I don't know that the jury can pick it up, but I see a bunch of certificates on the wall here that relate to some guy named Joel Jones.

A: Yes. We are using Dr. Jones' office.

Q: Why aren't we using your office, sir?

A: I—well—I really don't have an office yet—but I hope to get one soon.

Lesson: This witness was not calm and cool under fire. His demeanor suggests that he has something to hide or to be embarrassed about. If he has just joined the organization in question, he should have simply and directly stated so, without squirming, showing weakness, and appearing as though he has something to hide. This expert might not make a good witness in front of a jury.

GOAL 5: PROBE FOR REASONS OF POSSIBLE BIAS THAT CAN BE BROUGHT BEFORE THE JURY

The expert witness's credibility is a major issue in any trial. Indeed, in some trials, it is the most important issue in the case. One fundamental way to destroy an expert's credibility is to show that the expert is, or could be, biased against or in favor of a party in the case. This is a legitimate area of inquiry because bias is always relevant to the credibility of the witness. When you agree to become an expert witness in a case, you can expect to be closely questioned on the subject of bias. You must accept this as being an integral part of being an expert witness. If you do not want to be questioned under oath about potential biases, you should not agree to become an expert witness in the case. Areas of inquiry on the subject of bias commonly include expert witness fees and income, the propensity for testifying only for plaintiffs or defendants, and any personal interest in the subject matter of the litigation or the individual or corporate litigants.

Example 2.8
Q: Sir, you are being paid a fee for the time and the services you are providing in this case, are you not?
A: Yes. I'm sorry.

Q: Does the fact that you're being provided a fee for your services affect the way that your opinion is going to go here today?

A: No, I'm provided a fee for other evaluations that I do.

Q: And sir, have you been asked to give evaluations both for plaintiffs and defendants in lawsuits?

A: Yes. (See pages 112-113 on bias.)

Q: The forensic psychiatric evaluations that you presently do, what are the sources of referral for those evaluations?

A: The sources of referral are attorneys or claims people from insurance companies.

Q: Of the forensic evaluations that you perform in civil matters, what percentage of those are for or in the behalf of plaintiffs?

A: I would estimate about 20 percent.

Q: Is the remaining 80 percent of referrals on behalf of defendants or insurance companies?

A: Yes.

Q: Have you ever criticized any consumer products as being defective?

A: Oh. Yes.

Q: What consumer products have you criticized as being defective?

A: In my entire life?

Q: Yes, to the extent that you can recall as you sit here right now.

A: I was highly critical with a case awhile back of a butane-fired cigarette lighter that would do a reasonable imitation of a flame thrower right out of the box.

Lesson: These are legitimate questions that are attempting to flesh out any potential biases of the deponents. The deponents did a good job answering these questions. They responded in a straight-forward, direct manner and did not appear evasive or as if they had something to hide.

GOAL 6: DETERMINE THE FACTUAL ASSUMPTIONS THAT ARE THE FOUNDATION OF YOUR OPINION

As an expert witness, your role in litigation is to offer an opinion relevant to one of the disputed issues in the case. Your opinion will always be based upon an assumed set of facts. For example, if you are a physician testifying as to the disability of a plaintiff, one of the factual assumptions you may have made is that the plaintiff was being truthful when she told you about her pain. Your opinion is only as good as the factual assumptions it is based upon. If opposing counsel can prove that the assumptions you made were incorrect, she may be able to damage the credibility of your opinion. The factual assumptions you have made in forming your opinion are therefore a legitimate area of inquiry at deposition and trial.

Example 2.9
Q: Your understanding then, Doctor, is that Todd Allen acted after the motor vehicle accident in precisely the same manner he acted before the motor vehicle accident and that is what you based your opinion on, correct?
A: Yes, that's what he described to me.

Q: Wouldn't you agree that it would be useful to take a look at their underlying evaluation sheets in order to really get a handle on the total feedback they received?
A: I think the summaries tell you what you need to know. If you want to look at more and more paper—
Q: How do you know that the summaries tell you what you need to know? Have you ever seen any evaluation sheets created by Yamaha's test riders?

A: No.

Q: How do you know and how can you be assured that riders didn't reach contrary conclusions that aren't included in the summary reports?

A: I guess I don't know that.

Lesson: These are good lines of questioning. Counsel has established that the witnesses have failed to consider potentially relevant information when forming their opinions. The second expert would have been better served had she read the underlying evaluation sheets.

GOAL 7: GATHER AS MUCH INFORMATION AS POSSIBLE

Counsel will attempt to gather as much information as possible about you and your opinion. Remember that you are obligated to answer truthfully the questions put to you. You are not, however, required to volunteer information and do counsel's job for her.

Included in counsel's attempt to gather information will be an attempt to educate herself on the science involved in your opinion. Questions concerning the science of your opinion serve a dual purpose. First, they educate counsel as to the underlying scientific principles or assumptions that you are using. Counsel can verify the validity of the scientific assumptions you are making with her own expert witness. Second, the questions help counsel get a better idea of how you may perform in front of a jury when attempting to testify about complicated technical matters. An expert witness is likely to perform well in front of a jury if he is capable of explaining complicated scientific or technical principles in terms a jury can understand.

Example 2.10
Q: What is an electronecessarystagnogram?
A: Nystagmus, N-Y-S-T-A-G-M-U-S, is the
movement of the eyes, involuntary movement. An
electronystagmogram is an electrical recording of that
movement of the eyes.
Q: What, of what clinical significance, if any, is that
test?
            Objection.
A: The nystagmus suggests that there is some
abnormality in the neural network going from the
vestibular, V-E-S-T-I-B-U-L-A-R, apparatus, the brain,
or the eyes.
Q: And if there is an abnormality on that test, what can
it signify?
A: It depends, of course, upon what part of that neural
network has been affected.

Lesson: Counsel may be sizing up the witness's ability
to explain complicated technical principles to the jury.

GOAL 8: USE YOUR OPINIONS TO HELP COUNSEL'S
CASE

Counsel will attempt to use your opinions in an attempt
to bolster his own case. This is commonly done in one
of three ways. First, counsel will attempt to point out
all the areas where you and the opposing expert are in
agreement. This is a useful technique because counsel
can then argue to the jury, "Even the defendant's expert
agrees that...." Often, this technique is used when
counsel cannot destroy your credibility by showing bias
or a lack of proper qualifications. Counsel may instead
choose to concede your credibility and point out the
many areas where your opinion supports her case.

Example 2.11
Q: You would agree with me, according to the classification system, the way you used it, that a grade II fracture has a higher risk of infection than a grade I fracture?
A: I would say that's true.

Lesson: Using the areas of agreement between the experts is an important technique to bolster the attorney's expert's credibility.

Second, counsel will attempt to show that if your underlying factual assumptions are changed to match the facts as the opposing side asserts exist, your opinion will change as well and support *their* case. Many experts will not give an inch in this area, but they should. You should realize, and the jury will certainly realize, that your opinion is only as good as the underlying factual assumptions, reports, correspondence, and test results upon which it is based. If those factual assumptions are changed, your opinion may very well change to be favorable to the other side. If true, you should readily admit that if you assume different facts then your opinion *may* change. Failure to readily do so may make you appear evasive and may damage your credibility. Remember, it is your role as an expert witness to provide your best, honest opinion based upon the information that has been provided to you. It is not your role to resolve all factual disputes in the case.

Example 2.12
Q: Let's assume for the moment that the test results from the lab were inaccurate. Given this assumption might you change your opinion?
A: Possibly, yes.

Lesson: The expert handled this question well. There is no point arguing that you will not change your opinion no matter what the facts are.

Third, counsel will attempt to push your opinion to the extreme in an attempt to make it look ridiculous.

Example 2.13
Q: And given what you know about the tendency of the vehicle to roll over and given what you know about the vehicle's handling characteristics, you think it's good design practice to have manufactured and sold three-wheel ATVs that could go as fast as 25 miles an hour for use by children as young as three years old?
A: Oh, yes.

Lesson: Extreme opinions may be difficult for the jury to believe. If counsel can push you into giving such an extreme opinion, she may lessen the weight that your opinion will have with the jury.

GOAL 9: INTIMIDATE THE EXPERT
Counsel may attempt to use the deposition as an opportunity to demonstrate to the expert the professional and personal price he or she will pay for continued involvement in the case. This price may be high as pointed questions about an expert's biases and qualifications (or lack thereof) are relevant to the

expert's credibility. Counsel may use such pointed questions during deposition with the additional goal of keeping the expert off balance and making the expert apprehensive about his or her upcoming trial testimony. An expert who is off balance during a deposition is more likely to let slip a hasty answer that has not been carefully thought out and that may be helpful to the opposition. An apprehensive expert is more likely to be unsure of herself and thus be a less credible witness at trial.

The way to deal with this goal of counsel is to accept at the outset of your engagement that pointed questions about your fees, biases, and qualifications are a legitimate and expected part of your participation in the case. The only way to avoid these questions is to decline to be involved as an expert witness. If you do choose to become involved as an expert, keep your cool during the deposition and don't provide any hasty or ill-considered answers.

Example 2.14
Q: Mr. Boyer, have you ever testified untruthfully?
A: I have testified on occasions and found that I had made a mistake.
Q: Could you tell me why Dick Wollin told the jury in the Weiner trial that you were an embarrassment to yourself and to Ford Motor Company?
A: I had run some tests that I found later were incorrect. The data I gathered was—I don't know whether it was accurate or not.
Q: And why did Mr. Wollin have to say you were an embarrassment to yourself and to Ford if it was an inadvertent mistake?
A: Well, I was extremely embarrassed when I found that I had made a mistake in what I testified to and sat

down on that evening, when I found the mistake, with Mr. Wollin and said, "I made a mistake here and it's something I shouldn't do. I'd like to recheck the data, recheck the testing, and present accurate information...."

Lesson: The expert did a good job of handling this difficult line of inquiry. By being forthcoming and readily admitting his earlier mistake, he has helped to mitigate the damage done to his credibility.

GOAL 10: LEARN AS MUCH AS POSSIBLE ABOUT THE OPPONENT'S CASE

Counsel will attempt to clarify and learn as much as possible about the opponent's side of the case. This will enable counsel to evaluate the settlement value of the case more accurately. It will also help counsel prepare for the possible trial of the matter.

Counsel will take the opportunity to be educated by the expert (i.e., learn things he or she may not have been able to otherwise discover). Experts are well advised not to succumb to the temptation to show how much they know and go out of their way to educate counsel.

> First, the plaintiff's attorney wants to learn as much about the subject matter as possible. You should explain that your expert need not educate the plaintiff's attorney any more than necessary to answer the questions truthfully. While you may want your expert to act as a teacher for the jury at trial, it is not necessary that the expert be a private tutor for the plaintiff's attorney.[1]

---

[1] Rex K. Linder, *Defense Counsel Journal,* Vol. 58, No.2 (April 1991) 175.

Friendly, open-ended questions playing to the expert witness's vanity and willingness to teach are used to obtain crucial information that may otherwise be unavailable to counsel. Don't give in to the temptation to provide more information than is asked for specifically.

Example 2.15

Q: How does weight distribution affect the handling characteristics of ATVs?

A: Well, weight distribution affects the development of the various forces that you're going to develop under various maneuvers under various terrains at the tires, which are part of developing, braking, acceleration and directional control. Weight transfer is a part of that, has to do with how that weight's transferred during various maneuvers, how the total design works in the weight transfer. And weight transaction is something that is a part of looking at little handling characteristics as well as a number of other factors.

Q: What other factors affect the handling characteristics of an ATV, other than weight distribution?

A: Power train design, acceleration characteristics, the nature of the tires, the nature of the suspension systems, operator location, operator movement, control inputs, position of the operator not only in movement but in terms of static sense. The nature of the interaction between the terrain and the tires. The attitude of the vehicle. There's a host of factors that go into handling. Those are just some of them.

Lesson: Counsel has pumped the expert dry of information and has invited further questioning. The witness would have been better served had he not responded so freely. Adding the phrase "as well as a number of other factors" invited additional questioning.

Example 2.16
Q: What lab values are inconsistent with a baby having metabolic acidosis at birth?
A: That's not what's important.
Q: Are there any lab values that are inconsistent with the premise that the infant had metabolic acidosis at birth?
A: Once you have a seizure, I think the relation becomes nonscientific and there's no point in even asking the question.
Q: You're going to have to explain that.
A: Once you have a seizure, it makes it impossible to tell anything. Any blood drawn after the seizure, in my mind, would make it impossible to tell anything about any occurrence before the seizure, because the seizure itself would change all the blood numbers. So now, you can't tell anything about anything before the seizure.
Q: So any lab values taken after the first seizure could not be utilized to determine whether or not the child had metabolic acidosis at birth?
A: That's my opinion.

Lesson: In this example, note how the expert has "corrected," "redirected," and then "educated" counsel on key elements in a medical malpractice case. He's doing counsel's job for her.

Example 2.17

Q: One method of determining the causative organism of a wound infection would be to do a swab culture with the caveat that you said earlier?

A: Right. It's a little dangerous and I've been told by the infectious disease people as well, they don't like to just swab the skin or the wound, because there's numerous bacteria on the human skin and you could have a false culture, may get a bacteria growing that's not actually causing the infection. It's recommended that you obtain a more direct culture from the fractured area, which is more invasive.

Q: The diagnosis for wound infection is based on, would it not be, your observations and the patient's report of any complaint of fever, chills, drainage, increased drainage, increased pain, odor coming from that area?

A: Again, it would be multifactoral. The patient's complaints and symptoms, the doctor's observations and any supportive laboratory findings or x-ray studies, given all that information and looking at that as one ball of evidence, if you will, then you can have the scale tipped one way or the other towards the....

Lesson: Better answers might have been to end each response after the first sentence. Counsel has the right to ask follow-up questions such as, "Is a swab culture the preferred way of determining the causative organism of a wound infection?" You should be careful about doing counsel's job for her.

Counsel's goals at a deposition will vary depending upon whether the deposition is a discovery deposition or a preservation of evidence deposition. The discovery deposition of an expert should help counsel prepare for trial. The expert's discovery deposition will also help each side to evaluate the settlement value of the case more accurately. To excel during depositions, experts need to keep in mind the goals of counsel explained in this chapter and the expert's role in the litigation.

Chapter 3 Preparing for Your Deposition

3.1 The Importance of Thorough Preparation

Experienced and sophisticated expert witnesses understand the need for complete and thorough preparation prior to being deposed. Your reputation and credibility are on the line. The attorney who will be examining you will most likely prepare thoroughly for the deposition. The best trial attorneys are not necessarily the smartest attorneys. They are usually the ones that work hard and prepare thoroughly. You must do the same if you want to excel during your deposition. The fact that you may be able to charge for your reasonable preparation time should remove any reason for not spending the time to become fully prepared.

The price of not being properly prepared may be high. Any oversights, mistakes, or errors you make due to a lack of preparation will become a permanent part of your "expert witness baggage." Not only is it likely to affect the result in the underlying case, but your future as an expert witness could be damaged permanently as well.

Example 3.1
Q: Okay. Mr. Coghill, have you ever been barred from testifying as an expert?
A: Well, let's see. Once in Virginia federal court.
Q: What was the name of that case?
A: Oh god. Something versus DESA Industries.
Q: Okay. It was a nail gun case?

A: Yes. You obviously seem to know about that one. So that, you know, that was—went up on appeal.
Q: And was reversed?
A: Reversed and retried.
Q: Any other cases?
A: And a case in Virginia where it was alleged that this—that relying on crash test data was hearsay evidence and that, therefore, I could not testify.
Q: Do you know the name of that case?
A: I can't remember that one.
Q: In how many other cases were you barred from testifying as an expert?

Lesson: What happens in one case that you are involved in can and will be brought up in subsequent cases. To do the best job possible in your current case you need to prepare thoroughly.

There is another important benefit of thorough preparation. That benefit is peace of mind. Giving an expert deposition can be a stressful experience. There may be much anxiety in the period leading up to the deposition. A great way to reduce this anxiety is to prepare thoroughly. Another benefit is that a prepared expert is less likely to make a mistake at deposition that can be used against her if she is later called upon to testify at trial.

3.2 How to Prepare

CONFERENCE WITH COUNSEL

Prior to being deposed, the expert should insist on a conference with the counsel representing the party who retained his or her services. Counsel may, in an attempt to save time and money, advise you that no such conference is necessary and that he or she will come "a few minutes early" to the deposition to talk things over. While this may be expedient for counsel, it will almost always result in inadequate preparation for you. This type of last-minute review is a recipe for disaster and you should refuse to participate in it. You need time to organize your file and your thoughts. Insist on a separate appointment with counsel prior to the date of the deposition.

At the pre-deposition conference, counsel should discuss with you any areas or issues with which you are concerned. These include the following.

1. The type of questions that you will be asked by opposing counsel. In complex or challenging cases, it is not unusual to have a "run-through" with a vigorous cross-examination by counsel or an associate. Here you will be asked the most difficult questions and be given an opportunity to reflect on the questions and answers.

2. The questions (if any) retaining counsel will ask you.

3. The pertinent legal standard for liability and causation. Review jury instructions.

4. Identifying any privileged information or work product contained in your file.

5. A review of what you should and should not bring to the deposition, including your response to any subpoenas you may have received.

6. An update on the current status of the litigation by sharing with you documents, interrogatories, and pleadings. If these are not forthcoming, you may request them so

that you can review them prior to your deposition.

7. A sharing with counsel of any prior contrary opinions you may have rendered in other cases.

8. A review of your qualifications with a discussion for the bases for your opinions and how they fit into the case.

Completion of such a pre-deposition conference will have many benefits. First and foremost, you will be given a fairly good idea of the types of questions you may be asked. You will also be updated on the status of the case and will have counsel review the applicable legal standards and "magic words" that must be utilized when giving your opinion. Finally, you will have an opportunity for counsel to review your file prior to it being produced at the deposition (if it has been subpoenaed).

Example 3.2
Q: Doctor, do you have an opinion as to whether or not the claimant's carpal tunnel syndrome was related to her employment?
A: Yes, I do.
Q: And what is that opinion?
A: To a reasonable degree of medical certainty, her carpal tunnel syndrome is related to her employment.

Lesson: During the pre-deposition conference, counsel may have reminded the witness that in order to be legally sufficient, her testimony needs to be based on "a reasonable degree of medical certainty." The conference may have helped prevent the witness from stating something such as, "I think it's related."

There is a downside to your pre-deposition conference with counsel. Opposing counsel can and will inquire about the meeting and what was and was not discussed. Skillful counsel will attempt to turn a legitimate pre-deposition conference with counsel into a nefarious activity with conspiratorial overtones. You should not be defensive or evasive when asked about meeting with counsel prior to the deposition to discuss the facts of the case and your opinions. This is a legitimate activity that will most likely also be used by the opposing side and its own experts. If your responses to questions about meetings with counsel are defensive, you will play into opposing counsel's hands. However, if you are not defensive about having met with counsel, the significance of the meeting will most likely be downplayed.

Example 3.3

Q: First of all, sir, are you here as a fair and impartial witness?

A: Yes.

Q: You indicated to Attorney Cochran that you don't care about the outcome of the case one way or the other?

A: Right.

Q: Okay. Would you explain to the jury why you met with Attorney Cochran behind closed doors for forty-five minutes before you gave testimony today?

A: I generally do that. He requested to meet with me and, and I did that.

Q: Well, you were informed by your staff that I had arrived for the deposition, correct?

A: Yes.

Q: And you did not invite me in, did you?

A: No, I did not.

Q: During that private conference, you and Attorney Cochran had conversations about this case?

A: Yes.

Q: Please detail for the jury what you and Attorney Cochran discussed behind closed doors for forty-five minutes immediately prior to this video deposition taken in lieu of live testimony, sir.

Lesson: This is a common and legitimate area of inquiry. The witness did a good job in not being evasive or defensive about the meeting. A truthful answer to the last question might be, "We discussed the procedures that will be used, the probable completion time of my testimony, and the probable questions I would be asked."

Example 3.4

Q: The report that you prepared that's dated February 17th, 1997, were there any drafts of that report prepared?

A: No, I mean other than—I don't know what a "draft" is but I use a word processor; so, if there was a draft it was destroyed in the process of preparing it. I don't think there were any other copies.

Q: Was there any other version sent to Mr. Pirok other than the one dated February 17th?

A: May I see that?

Q: Yes.

A: Yes.

Q: Do you have a copy of the other version?

A: No, but I can tell you exactly what the difference was.

Q: Okay.

A: That paragraph after item No. 6 was added.

Q: The portion where you say you would like to reserve the opportunity to amend your opinions?
A: Right.
Q: Was that inserted at the suggestion of counsel when you met with him?
A: Yes, I'd have to say he and I—
Q: He pretty much offered that paragraph for you?
A: I wouldn't say that. He said he had these other depositions which were referred to in my earlier correspondence that I was supposed to be reviewing and I hadn't received them yet. And so he said wait up on that until after I send you those depositions, but he had already committed to sending them to me prior to that particular day; so, yes, the answer is he wanted me to be sure to look at those.

Lesson: You need to be prepared to testify about what was said and done during the pre-deposition conference with counsel.

Your Curriculum Vitae

You can and should expect to have the contents of your CV carefully probed at deposition. As part of the preparation process, it is crucial for experts to update and fact-check the accuracy of their CVs carefully. Failure to do so can result in needless damage to your credibility that could have been easily avoided through proper preparation.

If your CV has been subpoenaed, you will be required to bring it with you to the deposition and produce it to counsel. Experts should be very cautious about having multiple versions of their CV (e.g., long ones, short ones, and worst of all, different CVs that emphasize different aspects of their experience and expertise). Skillful counsel can and will portray this as an attempt to slant the CV to curry favor with the party who is considering retaining you.

Example 3.5

Q: Did you bring a copy of your curriculum vitae here today?

A: Yes, I did.

Q: The CV that you handed me dated February 1, 1998, is this your current CV?

A: Yes.

Q: Do you know when the last time was that you updated your CV?

A: February 1, 1998.

Q: Since that time, you have published, correct?

A: Yes.

Q: Since February 1, 1998, you have lectured, correct?

A: Yes.

Q: Are these reflected in your CV?

A: No...I guess I really should update it.

Q: What other activities are not reflected in your February 1, 1998, CV, sir?

A: Well....

Lesson: Failure to take the simple step of updating his CV has caused the witness to needlessly lose credibility.

Example 3.6

Q: Did you bring a copy of your resume with you today?

A: No, I didn't.

Q: Well, I knew that was your practice, Mr. McDonald, not to bring it, so I brought one for you.

Lesson: Experts who decide to be clever and leave their CVs home can anticipate this type of exchange.

Example 3.7

Q: You have several different versions of your CV, do you not?

A: Well, I have a complete CV and a shortened version for faxing.

Q: I show you four different versions of your CV dated 1998. Are these your CVs?

A: Yes.

Q: Isn't it a fact that you have a "defense" CV you send to insurance companies and a "plaintiff" CV you send to plaintiff's counsel, sir?

A: No...well I do have different CVs which emphasize different....

Lesson: Having "defense" and "plaintiff" CVs should be avoided. If this is discovered, you will appear to be for sale to the highest bidder and your credibility will be lessened.

REVIEW THE IMPORTANT DATES

Successful expert witnesses review the crucial dates in the case. Many commit them to memory. These dates include the following.

- When you were first contacted by counsel.
- When you were retained as an expert.
- When you received the records and from whom they were received.
- When you formed your opinion(s) in the case.
- The date of the accident in question.
- The date(s) key tests were performed.

Your accurate testimony regarding dates will greatly increase your credibility. Failure to keep the relevant dates straight will damage your credibility.

Example 3.8

Q: Do you know when you were first contacted by the attorneys for Manorcare?

A: No.

Q: Do you keep a log of phone contacts related to this case?

A: There would be a log on the scheduling book, but for the most part, there's not a date associated with that.

Q: Do you recall if you had any conversations with the attorneys for Manorcare before receiving the July 7, 1998, letter that you have in your file?

A: I can't recall any specific conversations....

Lesson: How much credibility do you think a jury will give to an expert who cannot keep his dates straight?

Example 3.9

Q: You don't know what date you dictated this report, do you?

A: It would have to be right around March 26th; I really don't know.

Q: You have no indication in the file as to the date?

A: No.

Q: And there is no signature on the file copy or the copy that I've been provided of the report which has your father's name?

A: I have not one in my file. I can't tell you if the original went to Creative Risk Management with a signature or to the Board or to Mumford.

Q: So there's no indication in your file that you ever reviewed this report of March 26th of 1992 after it was typed; isn't that right?

A: There's no notation of that....

Lesson: The failure of the expert to know when his report was dictated will lessen his credibility.

MASTERING THE IMPORTANT FACTS

You need to completely master the important facts of the case. You should know as much as possible about the facts of the case and should be prepared to discuss your opinions as well as those of the experts for the opposing party. Of course, you will need to possess an absolute mastery of your own opinions and reports.

Remember, your opinion is only as good as the facts upon which it is based. If you get the facts wrong during the deposition, your opinion may become worthless and your reputation and marketability as an expert witness may be severely damaged. The only way to master the facts of the case prior to deposition is to do your homework and thoroughly prepare.

Example 3.10

Q: You used the term "psychiatric or neuropsychiatric." What is the difference between psychiatric and neuropsychiatric?

A: I think neuropsychiatric usually would refer to some psychiatric problem that has a neurologic overlay or component. Neurobiologic.

Q: Is there a specialty in the field of psychiatry of neuropsychiatry?

A: No. Although, psychiatry is a part of—there's an American Board of Psychiatry & Neurology, you know, which accredits people in either specialty or both, but there is no—there is no specialty of neuropsychiatry per se. It's psychiatry and neurology.

Q: Would you say that you're a neuropsychiatrist?

A: I think so....

Lesson: This expert appears ill-prepared to answer counsel's questions.

Example 3.11

Q: In the Szabo test, how many exposures had a delta-V in excess of 6.1 miles per hour?

A: If you can direct me to it, that would save me a little bit of time.... I'm sorry. I think I have it. Page 301?

Q: I think so.

A: Vehicle kinematics. The impact velos—well, I got the impact velocity for delta-V. I'm doing the calculation in my head. What is the number? I should have brought a calculator. Would appear only two of those tests were over the—that produce a delta-V of higher than 6.1 miles per hour.

Q: Which two are they?

A: Those are the two that are listed as kilometers per hour of 10. The 9.6 kilometers per hour is just about 6 miles an hour, so it's not quite 6.1.

Q: Okay. Can you tell me with regard to those two collisions in excess of 6.1 miles per hour, how many test subjects?

A: Well now I'm trying to figure out which test subjects were in which test.

Q: Let me ask you, when you told me that there were two, you were looking at Table 3?

A: Yes.

Q: Under delta-V?

A: Correct.

Q: Okay. If we go over to the left, there's five—there's two sets of five tests with the letters A through E.

A: Okay.

Q: Do we presume that the first test that was 10 was subject D and the second test was subject A?

A: Probably.

Q: Okay.

A: Without checking the rest of the paper to be sure of that, it would appear to be that way, but I'm, you know....

Lesson: The expert must know her own reports cold. This expert did not and thus was a less valuable witness.

REST AND RELAXATION

You should come to depositions well rested. In addition, your anxiety level can be reduced by making sure you leave adequate time to be deposed. If the lawyers tell you it will take two hours, plan on four to be safe. Nothing is worse than a lawyer recognizing that an expert is time-pressed to finish his or her testimony. If counsel recognizes this, she may use it against you in an effort to have you concede contested points.

3.3 What to Do If You Are Not Properly Prepared

Adequate preparation is essential for proper performance during depositions. A failure to properly prepare may result in needless mistakes that will damage your credibility and reduce your marketability as an expert witness in future cases.

The question arises as to what to do if you and the attorney do not have time to properly prepare. The authors have two recommendations. First, find the time. Make preparation for the deposition a priority and insist that counsel take the time to talk with you prior to the deposition. This meeting can be done over the phone if necessary. Second, have the deposition rescheduled. *Depositions are very commonly rescheduled or "put over" for illness, scheduling conflicts, and even for no stated reason at all.* If you do not feel prepared for a deposition or do not have time in the days leading up to it to adequately prepare, ask that your attorney attempt to reschedule it. It is likely that she will be able to do so. It is more likely that she will be able to do so the earlier you ask for the rescheduling. Depositions are scheduled by the parties and are often rescheduled. Don't be afraid to ask the counsel who retained you to attempt to reschedule the deposition if you feel this is necessary.

Chapter 4 Subpoenas, Subpoenas Duces Tecum, and the Use of Documents at Deposition

4.1 The Subpoena

Depositions for expert witnesses are often scheduled by the attorney serving the expert with *a notice of deposition.* This legal document will specify the name of the case and give the time and date of the deposition. In many cases a subpoena to appear will also be served on the deponent. One of the reasons that counsel issues a subpoena is to protect himself. If an expert witness is not served with a subpoena and does not show up at a deposition, counsel can be liable for court costs including attorney's fees.[1]

FAILURE TO APPEAR

Expert witnesses who receive a deposition notice and subpoena and fail to appear at their deposition may subject themselves to court costs, counsel fees, contempt of court charges, and in rare instances, suit for malpractice or negligence. Federal Rule of Civil Procedure 45(e) dealing with subpoenas provides, "Failure by any person without adequate excuse to obey a subpoena served upon that person may be deemed a contempt of the court from which the subpoena issued...."

As a practical matter, as soon as the expert witness becomes aware of the fact that he or she cannot make the deposition due to conflicts, illness, inclement

---

[1] Fed. R. Civ. Pro. 30(g)(2).

weather, family emergencies, etc., the expert should notify both counsel who has retained him or her and counsel who has issued the subpoena. In most cases, the deposition will be rescheduled without difficulty. The major exception is when counsel is up against a court-ordered time deadline. Deadlines may make postponement difficult for all parties.

The expert witness who does not note his calendar and fails to appear at deposition will incur the wrath of both counsel who has retained him and opposing counsel. The expert may be liable for stenographic costs and reasonable attorney's fees. If, due to time deadlines or discovery schedules, counsel is not permitted to reschedule the expert's deposition and loses the case, the expert may be liable for negligence or professional malpractice. It is a good idea to have the home phone number of counsel should emergencies arise. Note that the expert witness who shows up late or makes the attorneys wait acts unprofessionally and detracts from his value as an expert.

4.2 The Subpoena Duces Tecum

In many cases, a subpoena of the type that requires the production of certain items will accompany the notice of deposition. This type of subpoena is a *subpoena duces tecum*. The subpoena duces tecum is a very powerful discovery tool because it forces persons or parties who are not parties to the lawsuit to "produce and permit copying and inspection of designated books, documents, or tangible things in the custody or control of that person."[2] Notice that the rule only provides that the person who is served with the subpoena permit them to be inspected and copied. The attorney is not

---

[2] Fed. R. Civ .Pro. 45(a)(1)(C).

allowed to retain the inspected original documents and books. Another limitation is that the documents must be in your "custody or control." You are not required to produce anything that is not in your "custody or control." These are legal terms and you should consult with counsel for advice regarding what they mean.

The "designated books, documents, or tangible things" are specified in an attached *schedule* or list. A sample of such a schedule has been provided in Appendix C.

You should have counsel review the documents that you intend to produce pursuant to the subpoena. Some of the information requested may be objectionable because it is privileged, a trial preparation document (attorney work product), or unduly burdensome. For example, you might be able to shield an attorney's request for production of your income tax returns.[3]

Experts who are served with a subpoena duces tecum are obligated to appear and produce the documents "as they are kept in the usual course of business or shall organize and label them to correspond with the categories in demand" in the schedule.[4] Thus, you are not allowed to intentionally disorganize the requested documents in an effort to make life miserable for the opposing attorney.

Many problems can arise for experts at deposition who are unfamiliar with the rules or who try to play "fast and loose" with documents in their possession or control. Such conduct is a serious error in judgment, can damage your reputation and credibility, and may result in civil and, in some cases, criminal penalties. An untruthful response to the

---

[3] See, e.g., *Hawkins v. South Plains International Trucks, Inc.* 139 F.R.D. 670 (D.Colo.1991).
[4] Fed. R. Civ. Pro. 45(d)(1).

simple question, "Is this your entire file?" could be perjurious if done intentionally.

What kinds of things will counsel look for in your file?

> The expert should be instructed to bring the entire contents of his or her file to the deposition. This can be done either by agreement with opposing counsel or by serving a subpoena duces tecum. Carefully review the original file maintained by the expert witness, paying particular attention to any notes or diagrams made by the witness, which may reveal his or her thought process. Copies of depositions or other file materials should be inspected page by page to see if the expert has made any notes, highlighting or other markings on these documents. These markings may provide important insight into what the expert views as significant supporting or damaging facts.[5]

4.3 Proper Handling of Documents at Deposition

PREPARATION

When you receive a notice of deposition and an attached schedule of documents to produce on a subpoena duces tecum, you should review the documents requested carefully. As previously discussed, some of the requested material may be objectionable. When you review the schedule and subpoena and bring all requested, nonobjectionable documents, you are responding appropriately and can answer questions about your file confidently.

---

[5] David R. Geiger, et. al, *Deposing Expert Witnesses* (Boston, MA: MCLE, 1993) 68.

Example 4.1

Q: I ask you to look at this notice entitled "Notice of Deposition." Have you seen any part of this notice before coming here today?

A: Yes, I have a copy of this.

Q: Do you see attached to that a Schedule A?

A: Yes.

Q: Was that given to you before you came?

A: Yes, it was.

(Stenographer marked Exhibit No. Three.)

Q: I will ask you to use your copy.

A: Sure.

Q: Before coming here today did you make an attempt to put together the materials that were requested on Schedule A?

A: Yes, I did.

Q: Have you brought with you notes that you prepared in the course of your inspection of the 480 DM Screener in the course of research on this case?

A: Yes, I have.

Q: Would you please produce those?

A: It's in this file right here and in this file right here.

Lesson: The deponent was forthcoming and responsive regarding the production of materials that the attorneys have a legal right to inspect under the discovery rules. He did not set off any red flags or warning bells by acting evasively.

Many experts unintentionally come to the deposition unprepared (i.e., without all of the documents requested). Needless stress, anxiety, and in some cases, continued depositions result from this lack of preparation.

Example 4.2

Q: May I see your file, Doctor?

A: Sure.

Q: Also, for the record, Doctor, you said there were certain x-rays that are available but not here?

A: From the original; those would be from the original visits, '86 and '88, I believe.

Q: Could you find those for me?

A: I can ask them to pull them. I don't know if I can find them. I'll have the other people look for them.

Q: Is she getting those x-rays, Doctor?

A: She's looking for them, yes. She had to pull up the number and everything.

Q: Do you know how long it will be?

A: I don't have a clue. In my office it would be about two minutes, but here I can't tell you.

> **Opposing Counsel:** Counsel, can we meet on Wednesday, then, July 31st at 10:00 A.M.?
> **Retaining Counsel:** Yes, I think I can be here.

Lesson: A few minutes of preparation could have avoided needless delay and having to come back for a continued deposition.

In some cases, experts are careless and produce documents in their file relating to *other* cases. This is a needless error that can be avoided with proper preparation. Consider the following example.

Example 4.3

Q: Professor, in this case have you brought your entire file with you?

A: I have.

Q: I see a letter from Mr. Kirok to Dan Hernan regarding the case *Browning versus Chicago and North Western.* Are you an expert in that case?

A: That doesn't belong in that file. I don't know how it got in here.

Q: But the question is: Are you an expert in that case?

A: Yes. Can we put that aside so that I can separate it out of there?

Q: Sure. Have you testified in that case yet?

A: No.

Q: Is your deposition scheduled in that matter?

A: Not that I'm aware of.

Q: Some more correspondence regarding Browning. From Linda Coyle of the UP, two of them, those have nothing to do with this case, right?

A: They do not, yes.

Q: Did you bring with you your file today?

A: Yes.

Q: I know we started kind of plowing through some of the stuff you brought. I have in front of me a book, *Repetitive Motion Disorders of the Upper Extremity* by, it looks like, edited by Steven L. Gordon, Sidney Blair and Lawrence Fine. Did you rely on this book in reaching any of your opinions in this case?

A: Yes.

Q: I also have *Work-Related Musculoskeletal Disorders, a Reference Book for Prevention* with various and assorted authors of which Hagberg and Silverstein leap right out at me. Did you rely on any portions of this book for your opinions in this matter?

A: Yes.

Q: You also gave to me a looseleaf, I don't know if you'd call it that, binder, "Office Ergonomics, Preventing Musculoskeletal Disorders" from a seminar this past month, this pink book. Have you relied on any of the materials in this in reaching your opinions?

A: My opinions were, as reflected in the report that I prepared, were prior to this document; so, no, I did not.
Q: This is just interesting reading material, right?
A: Well, it may have affected my opinion since the last time I read the report, which is a period of time ago.

Lesson: When preparing, make a final check of the file to make sure only documents that have been requested are in the file to be produced. Documents that have not been requested that pertain to other cases should not be left in the file.

DEALING WITH EXHIBITS

The attorneys who question you about documents usually will have those documents *marked* for identification. This usually involves the placing of a small sticker on the document in question. This sticker will contain a number or letter or both such as "P-1" and would thereafter be referred to as *exhibit P-1*. This is done for identification purposes in order to clarify the record (transcript) of the deposition. It has nothing directly to do with the admission of the document in question into evidence. Because exhibit nomenclature can often get confusing, you should always try to double check that the document you are referring to is the one the attorney is asking you about. Failure to take this simple precaution could result in your giving confused and erroneous testimony that can be used against you at trial. If such testimony is given, the record may not reveal that you were looking at the wrong document when you were asked the crucial question.

Example 4.4

Q: Let me refer your attention to defense exhibit 17A. Do you agree with the conclusions set forth in this report?

A: Just to be sure which report we're talking about, is that the four-page EPA Site Report dated July 21, 1998?

Lesson: The simple precaution of verifying the identity of the document in question and reading this verification into the record helped prevent the expert from giving potentially erroneous testimony.

TAKE YOUR TIME

When you are questioned about a document at deposition, ask to take the time to read it and review it carefully before you answer any questions. Do not concern yourself with the fact that you are slowing down the deposition or that counsel is getting impatient. That is the attorney's problem, not yours. If the deposition is not being videotaped, the time that you take reviewing the document will *not* be reflected in the deposition transcript. Because the transcript is what matters most, your careful review of the document in question is likely to have no downside.

Example 4.5

Q: Have you seen this document marked exhibit #3, answers to interrogatories?

A: No.

Q: With reference to question and answer #4, will that be your opinion at trial?

A: I will need some time to read and review the document.

Lesson: The expert asked to read the entire document, not just question and answer #4. Reading the entire document is always recommended to ensure understanding the context of various parts of the document.

HANDWRITTEN NOTES

Experts are frequently questioned at length about underlining, highlighting, and margin notes that appear in their files. Experienced experts have learned not to make such notations. Some experts even make it a routine practice to discard, as an ordinary and customary business practice, any preliminary notes that were made once a final report has been issued. This is often done because the preliminary notes are no longer needed once the final report has been issued. Discarding notes would not be ethical or legal if these notes were under subpoena at the time they were discarded. Furthermore, the discarding of notes can be a topic of examination at deposition. If notes are not discarded in every case as an ordinary and customary business practice, counsel may be able to make a strong argument to the fact finder that these notes were intentionally discarded in an effort to hide something.

Example 4.6

Q: Sir, I note that within this package, there is some blue underline. And I'd like to show you on a handwritten note of December 2nd, 1985, there is some blue underline, and ask you if you know who made those underlines.

A: I did.

Q: Why did you underline this particular passage?

Q: You've got the deposition of JoAnne Jones and again you've underlined, even dog-eared some things

regarding her symptoms, when she started to work.
Maybe I better let you look at that. Is there anything in
that deposition that you've highlighted that you feel
pertains to your opinions beyond when she started to
work, her age and her symptoms?

A: No. I think that probably summarizes it.

Lesson: Be very careful about any handwritten notes
or highlighting that you place on documents. You will
almost always be questioned closely about such notes at
deposition or trial.

PRIVATE NOTES

Some experts mistakenly believe that their notes are
"private" and should not have to be disclosed. *There is
simply no such thing as far as the law is concerned as
a "private note" privilege.* Notes can and will be
discoverable as long as no exceptions to the discovery
rules apply (e.g., privilege, attorney work product,
undue burden, etc.). The only way to guarantee that a
note is never produced for discovery is to never create
that note in the first place.

Example 4.7

Q: Now, your file or a file related to this is comprised
of the two deposition transcripts and the offer of proof;
is that correct? Is this one of the documents provided to
you by Risk Management, the offer of proof?

A: Yes.

Q: And the rest of the documents are medical records
provided to you by Risk Management?

A: Yes.

Q: Have you in preparation for today's depositions,
apart from what you said about the two depositions,
have you reviewed the medical records?

A: Yes.

Q: In addition to the medical records, do you have some notes related to this case?

A: I have one page of notes.

Q: Could I see those?

> **Mr. Perna:** Could I just look at them first? (Pause.)
> **Mr. Perna:** Okay.
> **Mr. Klondike:** Let's mark this as Exhibit No. 4.

A: Am I not entitled to the privacy of my own notes? These are not for submission.

Q: Sir, your work related to this case, because it's involved in litigation, is available to me.

A: I would not describe this as work. This is my notes. If I were preparing these to be copied or submitted, I would certainly not submit them in this form.

Q: I understand.

A: This is just me, just in terms of a quick rundown. I'd be happy to type them without changing them, but—

> **Mr. Perna:** That's all right.

A: But that's certainly not representative of my style of work, to copy my scribbled notes.

Q: I understand. Are these notes that you made during your review of the case?

A: Yes.

Q: Could I see them, please?

A: Yes.

Lesson: The answer to the expert's question is no. He is not entitled to the privacy of his own notes. They must be produced.

ATTEMPTS TO HIDE DOCUMENTS

You can expect to be questioned closely about whether
anything has been removed from your file. Any
attempt by the expert witness to "sanitize" his or her
file is improper. Such an attempt will frequently make
the expert look bad in the eyes of the jury or fact finder.
A single act of removal of documents from a file can
completely destroy the credibility of an expert witness.
The problem of removal of documents is exacerbated if
the removal is recorded on videotape.

Example 4.8
Q: Sir, did you bring with you today your file
regarding the *Christie* case?
A: Yes.
Q: May I look at it, please?
A: (Witness proffers file to counsel.)
Q: In addition, sir, I see that you've placed some
documents on your desk. Are those documents
included as part of your file in your office?
Objection.
A: Yes.
Q: Could I see those, please?
A: (Witness reluctantly proffers to counsel.)

Lesson: The witness has damaged her credibility by
intentionally withholding information from the file.

Example 4.9
Q: Please give me your entire file.
A: I'm getting the part that you requested.
Q: I want—I'd like the whole thing, please. The
whole paper. I'll take the whole chart, in fact.
A: Here's the—

Q: Doctor, may I see your whole chart, please? I'm sorry. You just took some papers out in the presence— This is on film. Can you hand me the whole chart and the documents you removed from it?

Lesson: The witness's attempt to hide documents has been caught on camera for the jury to see and hear. This attempt to hide documents has needlessly damaged the witness's credibility.

COVER LETTERS

One of the most frequent areas of controversy is the "cover letter" the expert receives from counsel or the party retaining him or her. ***The cover letter is not protected by attorney-client privilege and, generally, must be produced.*** In many cases, the cover letter is very revealing to counsel. Counsel should be very careful when drafting these cover letters.

It is not uncommon for skirmishes to break out at deposition between counsel as to whether a cover letter is privileged and need not be produced by the expert. The attorney-client privilege does not act in most states to shield your communications with counsel. This is true because counsel is not representing you, she is representing someone else (the plaintiff or the defendant). When faced with claims of privilege and other evidentiary battles, the expert is well advised to do the following.

1. Let the lawyers sort out the dispute before turning over any documents.
2. Stay out of the dispute if possible.
3. Remember that counsel for the party who has retained you is *not* your lawyer and may be more concerned about winning the case than safeguarding your reputation.

Example 4.10

Q: Was there a—I see you showed me a whole stack of records and a whole number are records or references in your report. Did those records come to you with some type of cover letter from either Mr. McLaughlin, his office or Selective Insurance Company?

A: They usually do come with a cover letter from the attorney's office.

Q: Can you find it for me?

A: This would be it. It's dated November 9, 1995.

Q: Now, in this letter—this letter was dated November 9, 1995, if we can have it marked P-1 for identification?

Q: Mr. McLaughlin indicates here in the letter that he's attaching a copy of Dr. Dunn's letter. Do you have any idea why it would not be in your file?

A: No, I don't.

Q: Has anybody asked you to remove it from your file?

A: No.

Lesson: By not having a complete file, the expert has given the attorney ammunition that can be used against the expert to lessen the expert's credibility.

Example 4.11

Q: Can you produce the cover letter which accompanied the documents you received?

> **Mr. Charles:** Objection. My transmittal letter to him is privileged as attorney-client—attorney work product.
>
> **Mr. Shafter:** Is this your client?
>
> **Mr. Charles:** It's attorney work product.
>
> **Mr. Shafter:** Didn't you include this letter to the doctor? How can you claim attorney work product after you disclosed it to an independent

expert? What's the basis of asserting that privilege?

Mr. Charles: My communication to the doctor as an expert witness is not subject to discovery.

Mr. Shafter: Under what basis, sir? This is a witness that you have disclosed. This is not an independent consultant. You're now asserting a privilege here. What's the basis of that?

Mr. Charles: My basis is that you're not entitled to see anything other than what he's referred to.

Mr. Shafter: Mr. Charles, on the basis that this is a consultant, that your work product is included in his chart, your work product is in his chart?

Mr. Charles: Yes.

Mr. Shafter: Is that what you're telling this judge?

Mr. Charles: Yes.

Lesson: The expert was well advised to stay out of the attorneys' privilege discussion.

Any letters of transmittal that you received when you were originally contacted or when records where forwarded to you can become a significant issue at deposition. Generally, these letters are a legitimate area of inquiry and need to be produced if subpoenaed. Attempts to play "hide and seek" with these letters is both unethical and unwise and can result in sanctions.

Example 4.12

Q: Doctor, if there's a transmittal letter on the cover, I'd like that included, too, please. Doctor, would you hand it over to me, please?

A: This is the file.

Q: Would you please hand me the papers that you've just taken out of your chart?

A: I gave you the file. This is just a letter from counsel.

Q: Did you give me back the papers that you took out?

A: Yes, I did.

Q: Now, Dr. Erick, have you given me your entire file including the transmittal letter?

A: Yes.

Q: Dr. Erick, I have before me Plaintiff's Number 1, which is an eighteen-page letter that you have taken out of your chart; is that correct?

A: I only took it out of the chart because...

Q: Yes or no, did you take it out of your chart?

A: I merely removed it from the chart to review it...I had no intention of....

Lesson: Cover letters are generally a legitimate area of inquiry. As such, attorneys and experts need to be very careful regarding what is placed in them. Attempts to be defensive about and conceal cover letters will most likely be counterproductive.

BILLING INFORMATION

You should anticipate that counsel will look for information on fee schedules and the expert's bill for the case. Some experts may fail to include this information in the file they produce, even if it has been specifically requested. Sophisticated counsel can make the failure to include this information look like a pattern of deceit. Remember that information regarding your fees is discoverable because it may indicate bias. There is no point in trying to hide this information. Remember also that juries know and understand that expert witnesses are paid for their time. Finally, remember that the expert witness retained by the opposing side is also being paid for his or her time. The fact that you are being paid will usually not taint your testimony.

Example 4.13

Q: Doctor, I would just like to, if you don't mind, have a look at your chart, because you've referred to it. Did you bring everything that you have relating to your work on this case here with you today?

A: Other than the x-ray films, yes.

Q: Okay. Are there other papers somewhere else in another file, in another office, that relate to the work that you did on Mr. Jones' case on behalf of this employer?

A: Not that I'm aware of.

Q: So, why don't you show that to me, if you don't mind.

A: (Handing the file.)

Q: Doctor, have you now just handed me your complete chart, as you know it, as it relates to Ronald Jones?

A: As I know it, yeah.

Q: Okay. (Reading.) Now, Doctor, as I look through this chart here, I'm not sure that I find any billing information from you. Is your billing information kept somewhere different?

A: That's not something that I am involved with in my practice.

Q: That wasn't my question. Is your billing information kept somewhere different?

A: I presume so, because it's not in the chart.

Q: So, in fact, you haven't brought everything that you have related to Ronald Jones here today. Do you want to change your answer that you gave me before?

A: Would you re—could I re-hear the original question again, please?

Q: Doctor, I asked you five minutes ago if you brought everything that you have as it relates to the work that you did on Ronald Jones, right? Remember that question?

A: Well, I remember that you asked me a question. I don't remember the exact wording that you used. I'd like to hear that again. Do I have a right to hear that?

Q: Doctor, did you bring everything—I'll ask it again. Did you bring everything that you have—

A: And I asked you a question, Mr. Shafter. Do I have a right to hear your question read back to me by the court reporter or not?

Q: No, Doctor. I'm asking you the question, and I'm going to keep going, and I'll rephrase it if you don't understand it. And maybe I should stop myself. If you don't understand one of my questions, would you tell me that? And I'll do my best to rephrase it.

A: All right. I will.

Q: Okay. But the question I asked was: Did you bring everything that you had as it relates to the work that you did on Ronald Jones? Do you remember that?

A: Yes.

Q: And you told me that you did, right?

A: I told you that I brought everything that I had available, yes.

Q: Now, I've looked in your chart, and I don't find any billing information.

A: That's right, you didn't.

Q: That's kept somewhere else?

A: I would presume so, yes.

Q: But you don't know?

A: But I don't think it has anything to do with the medical part of this case. The fact that a billing record is not kept in the chart has very little to do with my opinion.

Q: Doctor, my question was: Did you bring everything that you have as it relates to him? And it appears that you did not, right?

A: I didn't bring the billing information, no.

Q: Okay. Do you have all the correspondence in that file?

Lesson: The witness has caused himself much difficulty by his failure to bring the billing information and his inability to admit this directly.

Chapter 5 Answering Counsel's Questions

To excel during expert depositions, you must be able to answer counsel's questions directly and truthfully without making mistakes or falling victim to counsel's tactics, traps, or trick questions. The best way to do this is to anticipate and prepare for questions that you will likely be asked. A forewarned expert deponent is a forearmed expert deponent. While you cannot prepare for every tactic that counsel may come up with, successful experts are able to deal with the lines of questioning that are used time and time again. This chapter will identify and give examples of the most common lines of questioning that have not been otherwise covered in this text. The expert witness who is aware of the common lines of questioning and tactics employed by counsel is in the strongest position to succeed at deposition. When reading this chapter, the expert should keep in mind the goals of counsel at deposition—to observe; to learn; to be educated; to pin down the expert's opinion; to challenge the expert's qualifications, expertise, methods and bias; and to discredit the methodology employed by the expert. You should also keep in mind that the rules of civil procedure allow for broad-based discovery in an effort to facilitate settlement and to eliminate unfair surprises at trial.

5.1 When the Case Was Accepted

Experts who are retained long after the accident or incident can expect to be questioned closely by counsel on this point. Counsel may be trying to get the jury or fact finder to believe there was a sinister reason for the delay. Alternatively, counsel's motives could include attempting to show that you did not have adequate time to perform a thorough analysis and/or that counsel was shopping the case around and having difficulty finding an expert to take the case. Another reason for the use of this line of questioning is to attempt to show that your analysis may be flawed because the subject of your analysis has changed or deteriorated during the time between the incident in question and your retention.

To excel during your deposition, you need to be prepared to deal with these types of questions. Do not attempt to be evasive about dates. These are hard facts and there is no role for evasiveness when asked a concise and direct question regarding the date you were first contacted or the date you first reviewed evidence in the case. To truly excel, you also need to prepare justifications (if they exist) as to why your analysis was not biased or flawed as a result of the date of your retention and analysis. Without forethought, these justifications and rationales may slip your mind at a crucial point in your deposition.

Example 5.1
Q: Mr. Floyd, would it be correct to say that you were not retained as an expert in this case until some 11 months after the accident occurred?
A: I was brought into this case I believe I said in....
Q: March of 1995?
A: That's correct.
Q: And your understanding is this accident occurred in April of 1994?
A: April 30th of '94, yes.
Q: So it was approximately an eleven month or ten month interval?

A: That's correct.

Q: As a rule, do you think it's desirable as an expert evaluating a piece of machinery to look at the piece of machinery fairly close in time or as close in time as possible to the event that you are investigating?

A: Yes, it is.

Q: You said you read the complaint in this action so you know the complaint was filed in this case in September of 1994?

A: If that is correct.

Q: Do you know why you were not retained until some six months after the complaint was filed?

A: No, I do not.

Q: Are you aware of any other experts who have been retained previously by ARCO Products prior to your coming in to the case?

A: No, I don't.

Q: You have no information on that at all?

A: No.

Q: Why is it desirable to be called into a case so soon after an incident as possible, sir?

A: Well the machinery is in the same condition, the grounds and conditions would be as similar as is possible.

Q: A lot might have happened to the machine in the intervening 11 months if it was in use, correct?

A: Yes.

Q: Was the machine in use during the intervening 11 months?

A: Yes, that's my understanding.

Q: How many hours of use and what maintenance and modifications did the machine undergo between April 30, 1994, and March 1995?

Lesson: The expert properly admitted that it would have been better to be called in earlier. This is obvious to most people (and most jurors) and there in no point in trying to split hairs. Counsel is planting the seeds of doubt in the mind of the jury about why there was a delay in calling in the expert. The jury is left to speculate. Note as well that counsel attempts to discover the existence of any consultants who have not been disclosed as experts. (See pages 6-7 on consultants versus testifying experts.) The expert's only possible mistake was in agreeing with counsel's characterization of "a lot" in the third-to-the-last question. Instead of accepting this broad characterization, a better response might have been, "There may have been some changes in the condition of the machine, yes." This response changes the response from yes, there could have been "a lot" of changes to yes, there could have been "some" changes. Both responses are truthful and accurate, but the latter one is much better in that it implies less change.

5.2 Qualifications

The expert should be prepared for counsel to use the deposition to discover and explore any weaknesses or shortcomings in his or her expertise, training, licensure, publications, experience, or certification. Because you are a witness in the case, your credibility is a legitimate and important issue. Your qualifications, or lack thereof, are relevant to your credibility and are an area where you can expect close questioning. To excel during depositions, you need to be prepared to handle these questions properly. If you are asked the question, "Doctor, are you board certified?," the answer is either yes or no. Evasiveness can be far more damaging to your credibility than an admission that you are not board certified because evasiveness may result in the perception that you are not honest. Also, keep in mind that your qualifications will be judged ultimately by a jury or other fact finder. *It is the authors' opinion that jurors are far more influenced by an expert's relevant practical experience, perceived honesty, and demeanor than the expert's academic record or lack of publications.* If the jury likes you, thinks you're honest, and feels that you have a good amount of relevant hands-on experience, you may be much more credible to them than an expert who is a professor with many publications, but who no longer does hands-on work and who has a pompous demeanor.

Example 5.2

Q: What is your occupation?

A: I am a mechanical engineer.

Q: What professional licenses do you possess?

A: I am not a registered professional engineer. I have a designation that is less than a professional engineering status…so, none.

Q: Again, do you have a license as an engineer?

A: No, I do not.

Q: What formal education have you had after high school?

A: I have a B.S. degree in mechanical engineering and I also have a Masters Degree in mechanical engineering.

Q: The B.S. in mechanical engineering was 1976 at the University of…Kentucky?

A: That is correct.

Q: Please tell us, what is mechanical engineering?

A: It's a course of study that broadly includes such topics as design, mathematics, heat transfer, fluid….

Q: Have you had any formal education in the nature of mechanical engineering or bioengineering since taking your Masters at the University of Kentucky?

A: No, I have not.

Q: Have you ever taken the test for an engineer's license in any state?

A: Yes, I have.

Q: Where was that?

A: In the State of Kentucky.

Q: Did you receive that license?

A: No, I did not.

Q: Why not?

A: I didn't pass the test.

Q: How many times did you take the test, sir?

A: Four.

Q: How many times did you fail the exam?

A: Four.

Lesson: The expert did not try and hide his lack of a license. Counsel who has retained this unlicensed expert has made a conscious and informed decision. After the expert has disclosed any professional shortcomings to retaining counsel, it becomes the problem of counsel and not the expert. Counsel and the expert may realize that demeanor, perceived honesty, and relevant practical experience weigh more heavily with the jury than the absence of professional designations or licensures that the jurors don't understand.

Example 5.3

Q: Doctor, have you ever attended a medical conference on head injury?

A: Not that I remember.

Q: Have you ever published an article on head injury?

A: No, I have not.

Q: Have you ever conducted any research on head injury?

A: No.

Q: Do you subscribe to any professional magazines or journals in the field of head injury?

A: No, I haven't.

> **Counsel:** Doctor, I want to thank you for your time.

Lesson: Note that the above physician, due to a lack of specific training and continuing education, may not have been well suited to testify about head injury. However, what wasn't asked was what the expert's experience with head injury had been. If this expert has been treating and diagnosing head injuries for forty years and appears believable and likeable, the jury may very well find her to be credible. Experts should, however, be cautious about being pushed by counsel into testifying in areas outside of their expertise. The expert's reputation, credibility, and standing in the profession are at stake.

CURRICULUM VITAE

You should anticipate that you will be questioned closely about your CVs. Counsel may try to show that you have been inconsistent or sloppy in putting together a CV. The lawyer will try to argue to the jury that they should not believe that the expert was accurate in her clinical methods and in formulating her conclusions and opinions if she was sloppy or inaccurate in formulating her own CV. Even a minor inconsistency in a CV can make a jury wonder why the expert has not corrected the CV. Is the expert lazy or just sloppy? If either conclusion is drawn by the jury, the expert will lose credibility. To prevent this kind of damage to your credibility, you need to review and correct your CV very carefully prior to deposition. (See pages 43-45 on reviewing your CV.)

Example 5.4

Q: Doctor, we were also provided what is Exhibit No. 2, a CV. Do you know how that differs from Exhibit No. 3 which also purports to be your CV?

A: It's an earlier—it's an earlier CV.

Q: Doctor, you would agree that there are marked inconsistencies between the 2 CVs?

A: Well, when we did the most current version, we were trying to shorten it—that's what most people want—the short version. So we did omit certain unimportant activities and articles.

Q: So the omissions were intentional, is that your testimony?

A: Yes, I just explained that.

Q: I'm directing your attention to Exhibit No. 3, the current CV. I ask if you would turn to page 4, your bibliography. Have you published other articles under your name in addition to the six that are listed?

A: Actually, yes. There's a letter to the editor of the New England Journal of Medicine, which is not included.

Q: What was the subject matter?

A: Writing of prescriptions. It's not relevant to the current topic.

Q: Didn't you write a textbook that is not listed?

A: Actually, it was a chapter in a textbook which outlined the diagnosis and treatment of infection in total hip arthroplasty.

Q: Did it discuss the diagnosis and treatment of a septic hip short of a revision of the implant?

A: It may have. I can't actually recall. It's 14 years ago....

Lesson: Counsel has taken a simple revision and shortening of a CV and made the expert look sloppy. In addition, counsel has raised the issue about why a key medical chapter was left off the CV.

Example 5.5

Q: Your CV states that you co-authored a paper entitled *Hand Truck Safety in the Work Place.* That was the *Modern Material Handling* magazine, April 1997. Who was your co-author on that paper?

A: John Mancini.

Q: I am a little confused in reading the curriculum vitae. I would like you to clarify for me, are you saying the paper was published in the April 1997 issue of *Modern Material Handling* magazine?

A: The paper was given at that date for a later publication.

Q: Was it ever published?

A: Yes.... As far as I know it was published in 1997. I think it was delayed for some reason.

Q: What issue?

A: I believe it was a, the, subsequent issue.

Q: Can you tell us what issue that was?

A: I don't recall specifically. I remember seeing the publication, I don't recall.

Lesson: When the expert's CV lists nonexistent or incorrectly cited articles, the expert's precision and credibility are quickly called into question. Was the assertion of publication a slip up, exaggeration, or lie?

5.3 Opinions

As an expert witness, your one and only reason for being allowed to testify is to give an opinion that will assist the trier of fact. You should anticipate close questioning concerning which opinions you will and will not be giving at trial. You should also expect close questioning about whether you are rigid and inflexible or if you would change your opinion if the facts are proven to be different. Counsel needs to know this information so that there won't be any surprises at trial. This information may also be helpful to counsel when she drafts pre-trial motions, such as motions for summary judgment.

Example 5.6
Q: Right. That was horseplay, wasn't it?
A: It didn't sound like it to me.
Q: If it was, that would change your opinion, though, correct?
A: No.
Q: Is your opinion etched in stone here today?
A: Etched in stone?
Q: Yes.
A: No. I know of few things that are etched in stone.
Q: Well, will you change your opinion?
A: Would I change my opinion?
Q: Yes.
A: Not at the present moment, no.

Lesson: The expert deftly deflected the attempt to portray his opinion as rigid (etched in stone) without actually changing his opinion. The expert did leave himself the option of changing his opinion at a later date.

Experts are often called upon to express their opinions during depositions and trials on crucial matters such as causation, negligence, disability, etc. Rule 702 of the Federal Rules of Evidence provides the basis for testimony by experts.[1] This rule has been widely adopted by the state courts.

When testifying at deposition, expert witnesses can anticipate and should prepare for an in-depth series of questions regarding their proposed opinions. The line of questioning will usually include the following areas of inquiry.

- The opinions the expert will be testifying to
- Any admissions counsel can elicit from the expert
- The facts and assumptions upon which the opinions are based
- The methodology employed in deriving the opinion
- When the opinion was first formed
- The deposition documents used by the expert in forming the opinion

---

[1] **Rule 702. Testimony by Experts**
If scientific, technical, or other specialized knowledge will assist the trier of fact to understand the evidence or to determine a fact in issue, a witness qualified as an expert by knowledge, skill, experience, training, or education, may testify thereto in the form of an opinion or otherwise.
NOTE: The Advisory Committee on state courts has proposed the following amendment to the Rule to reflect the changes brought about by the Supreme Court Case of *Daubert v. Merrell Dow Pharmaceuticals,* Inc. 113 S.Ct. 2786 (1993).
Rule 702. Testimony by Experts (Proposed)
If scientific, technical, or other specialized knowledge will assist the trier of fact to understand the evidence or to determine a fact in issue, a witness qualified as an expert by knowledge, skill, experience, training, or education, may testify thereto in the form of an opinion or otherwise - provided that (1) the testimony is sufficiently based upon reliable facts or data, (2) the testimony is the product of reliable principles and methods, and (3) the witness has applied the principles and methods reliably to the facts of the case.

- The degree of flexibility in the opinion (i.e., what would it take to get the expert to change his or her opinion)
- How the proposed opinion compares to answers previously given during discovery

STRATEGY

Counsel for the opposing party will probe to see if the expert's opinion can be undermined by challenging the underlying facts, assumptions, and documents relied upon. In addition, counsel will try to discover at deposition if the expert can be *turned;* that is, made to change his or her opinion if the underlying facts are modified slightly. Counsel will seek admissions and concessions that can be used at trial later. The expert who prepares thoroughly and rigorously and anticipates these attacks on his or her opinions usually excels at deposition.

OPINIONS THAT THE EXPERT WILL BE TESTIFYING ON DURING DIRECT TESTIMONY AT TRIAL

At deposition, expert witnesses may be questioned by counsel for the party who retained the expert. These opinion questions will usually be direct "softballs" that all parties expect the expert to answer simply and directly.

Example 5.7
Q: Now, Doctor, to a reasonable degree of medical certainty or probability—that is, is it more likely than not—based on the history you took, the physical examination you performed and the diagnostic studies you reviewed, did you form an opinion as to whether David Morgan suffered a herniated disc as either the

direct or proximate result of a work injury on or about
November 29 or November 30 of 1992?
A: Yes.
Q: And what is your opinion?
A: It is directly related to a specific injury at that time.

Lesson: The expert handled this softball well. He did
not overtestify. He avoided deftly the potential pitfall
of mentioning the date the accident happened.

Don't be overeager to proffer your opinion.
When an expert is overly eager to proffer an opinion,
her credibility and impartiality may be called into
question. Consider the following example.

Example 5.8
Q: Doctor, in this case, it is agreed that Ricky Murphy
had lumbosacral strain as a result of his injury at work.
The question that we have here today is whether the
injury at work resulted in a herniated disk. Do you
have an opinion?
A: Yes, it did.

Lesson: The doctor made two mistakes here. First, she
was too eager to give her opinion. This may make her
look biased and result in lost credibility. Second, she
answered more than what was asked. Her answer to the
question, "Do you have an opinion?" should have been,
"Yes, I have an opinion." It is counsel's job to follow
up with the question, "And what is that opinion,
Doctor?"

Counsel will also want to try to clarify and narrow the opinions that you are likely to offer at trial. Finding out which opinions you are not going to give may be as important to counsel as finding out which opinions you will proffer at trial.

Example 5.9
Q: To what extent, if you have an opinion as you sit here today, should Honda's engineers have consulted those recommended practices and standards in the design of its ATVs?
A: As I sit here, I don't have an opinion on the extent.

Q: Is it fair to say that you would not be proffering an opinion with respect to Frederick's outcome based on a review of the films?
A: I hope not to proffer any opinion about her films.

Lesson: In both of the exchanges above, note how the experts have not completely foreclosed the possibility of giving an opinion at a later date. These are truthful, yet artful, responses.

ADMISSIONS

Often, sophisticated counsel will, prior to attacking the opinions of the expert, obtain crucial admissions from him or her. This tactic serves two purposes. First, it may serve to bolster the opinion of the expert for the opposing party. Second, it narrows significantly the contested areas of inquiry.

Example 5.10
Q: Doctor, I'm going to ask a number of things about the opinion that you have just stated, and there, I believe, will be some areas where we have agreement

and some areas where we have some disagreement. I
would like to, if it's all right with you, find first some
areas of agreement, okay?.

A: Fine.

Q: You would agree with me that Mr. Allen suffers
from post-traumatic stress disorder?

A: Yes, I would.

Q: You would agree with me that post-traumatic stress
disorder is a real entity?

A: Yes, I would.

Q: You would understand that when I ask you that
question, there are persons in society that might think
that post-traumatic stress disorder doesn't exist?

A: Yes. I understand some people find it controversial.

Q: Okay. In your opinion, post-traumatic stress
disorder is a real psychological or psychiatric illness?

A: Yes.

Q: You would agree with me that Mr. Allen's post-
traumatic stress disorder has been exhibited through
classic signs and symptoms, correct?

A: Yes.

Q: Those classic signs and symptoms would be those
things as set out in the *Diagnostic and Statistical
Manual*, fourth edition, correct?

A: That's correct.

Q: That would be known as the DSM-IV?

A: Yes.

Q: Would I be correct in assuming that you have made
the diagnosis of post-traumatic stress disorder based on
criteria in the DSM-IV?

A: Yes.

Lesson: Here counsel has obtained crucial admissions
quickly and effectively from the expert. Counsel then
will go on to cross-examine the expert closely on the
"cause" of the post-traumatic stress disorder. The

expert understood and accepted the fact that the diagnosis was not really an issue and was compliant until the "cause" of the disorder was put in issue.

OPINIONS AND RATIONALE

Counsel will always attempt to determine what the expert testimony is likely to be and the rationale for the opinions of the expert. This information is critical if counsel is to prepare for trial and evaluate properly the settlement value of the case.

Example 5.11
Q: Do you have an opinion with respect to whether or not Bob Johnson was negligent in this case?
A: I guess I don't have an opinion one way or the other. I don't know enough about what dealers should or shouldn't do.
Q: In this case was Celena Navarro negligent?
A: Yes.
Q: How was she negligent?
A: One, for failing to wear a helmet. Secondly, from riding without direct supervision, which was my understanding, at least from her mother's deposition, was what the family rule was. And then lastly, for operating the vehicle in such a manner to allow herself to drift off the road on the right-hand side to an area where there clearly is a hazard in terms of the waterway and ditch, so she could either have driven slower or stayed away from that side of the roadway.
Q: Anything else?
A: No.

Lesson: Counsel has determined the expert's opinions and the reasons why she finds one party was negligent. Should the expert change her opinions or her rationale, counsel will be able to impeach her at trial by confronting her with the inconsistent testimony from the deposition.

FRONTAL ASSAULT

Frequently, counsel will open the deposition not with formal niceties or simple introductory questions, but with key questions on the expert's opinion and the underlying facts upon which the opinion is based. The expert must be prepared for this frontal assault. It is designed to catch you off guard and thus gain valuable admissions.

Example 5.12

Q: Good morning, Mr. Perna. As you know, my name is Bruce Stein. I represent Earnest Drago with regard to this motor vehicle collision. It's my understanding that it's your opinion that the speed change of Mr. Drago's Saab was no more than 6.1 miles per hour; is that correct?

A: That is correct.

Q: As a result of that change of speed, the average forward acceleration of Mr. Drago's Saab was no more than 2.8 g's for a duration of approximately 100 milliseconds; is that correct?

A: That is correct.

Q: You used the term "average acceleration." What was the peak acceleration for Mr. Drago's Saab?

A: Well, I don't technically compute that; however, you would expect it to be approximately two point-two times the 2.8, or 5.6g's.

Q: Did you calculate the average or peak g's that were applied to Mr. Drago's neck or head?

A: No.

Q: Why did you not do that?

A: I'm working on the car rather than the person.

Q: Could you calculate the peak or average g's that were applied to Mr. Drago's head?

A: That's normally done by the biomechanist, in these cases, and not by me. And to be perfectly—I, you know, if somebody gave me the equation, yes, I could punch them in the calculator and compute them. But, no, I don't normally do that and I don't normally know those code equations.

Lesson: Counsel has established the expert's opinion and put him on the defensive almost immediately.

WHEN YOUR OPINION WAS FORMED

You may be asked when you formed each opinion in the case. The date of the opinion frequently has significance because it can affect what information and evidence the expert did and did not consider in forming the opinion. Often, counsel will attempt to develop a timeline to indicate that crucial data could not have been considered because it did not come into the hands of the expert until after the opinion was formed. Counsel may also attempt to show that crucial evidence may have been altered or was no longer available at the time the opinion was formed.

Example 5.13

Q: I want to know what information you had when you wrote this report in November 1995 with regard to it being a minor collision; not with regard to the neurologic findings, with regard to the severity of the collision.

A: There are other things which were relied on when other studies—initial studies, including MRIs were normal, he had an EEG done which was normal. All those things should be abnormal in a patient that has more severe injuries. All these would mean it was a mild injury.

Q: Can you just tell me, Doctor, what information you had with regard to how violent or nonviolent this collision was at the time that you wrote the report?

A: Just the things we talked about.

Q: Would it be fair to say that you had no information at the time that you wrote this report of November 1995 with regard to the speed of the vehicles involved in this accident?

A: To the actual speed? No, I did not.

Q: Do you know whether or not Mr. Framo's vehicle was stopped or moving?

A: No, I did not.

Q: Were you given any information from Mr. Framo or Mr. McLaughlin or any other source of how fast Ms. Small was going at the time her vehicle struck Mr. Framo's vehicle?

A: No.

Q: Do you know how much property damage there was to either Mr. Framo's vehicle or Ms. Small's vehicle?

A: No.

Q: So when you formed your opinion and wrote in your report in November 1995 that this was a minor collision, you had no information about the speed of either vehicle or the property damage to either vehicle. Correct?

A: Yes, that's right.

Lesson: The date the opinion was formed is important because counsel can and will attempt to point out the information that was not available to you when you formed your opinion.

YOUR OPINION AND OTHER EXPERTS

Counsel may attempt to discredit your opinion by showing that it is based primarily on the opinion of others. Sophisticated counsel will leave it to the jury or fact finder to conclude that the expert's opinion relies too heavily on conclusions reached by other experts. Relying on other experts' conclusions is allowed under the Federal Rules of Evidence,[2] but such reliance can and will be used to lessen the weight given your testimony.

Example 5.14

Q: What objective factors did you rely upon in coming to your opinion that he was malingering?

A: Well as I said, my opinion that he was malingering was based on my examination of my interview, my observations of him, and I think that my opinion was supported by Dr. Murphy's findings and those of Dr. Reiten.

Q: Did you rely on Dr. Murphy's findings in coming to your conclusion?

A: Well, relied in the sense that I read it and I put some reliance on it since I found it supportive. It was not the only factor in my forming that conclusion, but as I said, it was supportive of my opinion.

Q: If Dr. Murphy had concluded based on the neuropsychological testing that Mr. Framo had brain injury, would that have changed your opinion?

---

[2] **Fed. R. Evid.703 Bases of Opinion Testimony by Experts**
The facts or data in the particular case upon which an expert bases an opinion or inference may be those perceived by or made known to the expert at or before the hearing. If of a type reasonably relied upon by experts in the particular field in forming opinions or inferences upon the subject, the facts or data need not be admissible in evidence.

A: Well, that would be an entirely different situation.
Q: My question is had he done that, would that have changed your opinion?
A: Sure.

Lesson: If the expert's opinion is based on another expert's opinion, it is only as good as that expert's opinion. This is a legitimate area of inquiry.

Counsel may compare your opinion with those of the other experts in the case. When doing this, she may be trying to have the jury or fact finder conclude that your opinion may be wrong because the other experts came up with a different conclusion.

Example 5.15
Q: So I want to know, are you saying all his doctors are wrong in their diagnosis?
A: I would say that all of them are incorrect that believe, that think that he does have an organic brain syndrome, yes. I think my diagnosis is the correct one.
Q: All right. Dr. Silverbrook diagnosed a concussion two or three days after the accident. That's an organic injury, is it not?
A: Yes.
Q: Was he wrong when he diagnosed a concussion?
A: I don't know because that's a time frame that is far beyond when I examined him.
Q: He was seen by Dr. Gomez shortly after the accident, who diagnosed a postconcussion and postconcussion syndrome. Was Dr. Gomez incorrect when he made that diagnosis?
A: He may have been. I don't know.

Q: Okay. He saw Dr. Zwill, I believe, in 1993 or '94 and he made a diagnosis of organic brain injury. Was he incorrect at the time that he made the evaluation?
A: I do not know, but he made that diagnosis based on the history and the complaints offered by Mr. Framo.
Q: When Dr. Dalrymple saw Mr. Framo at Hampton Hospital, he made a diagnosis of partial seizure disorder. Was he incorrect when he made that diagnosis?
A: I don't know.

Lesson: Contrasting your opinion with that of several other experts can be an effective technique. Note also how counsel has been able to elicit a series of "I don't know" answers from the expert, which seriously call into question the validity of the expert's own opinion. If the expert doesn't know the answer to all these seemingly basic questions, how can he be so sure of his opinion?

INTERROGATORY ANSWERS

As part of the discovery process, counsel is allowed to propound written questions or *interrogatories* to other parties. These questions must be answered under oath. Included in almost all interrogatories are questions about the party's experts and their qualifications, opinions, and the factual bases for these opinions. A sample set of answers to interrogatories has been provided in Appendix B. You can expect to be questioned about the answers to interrogatories. As such, you should review them prior to the deposition. Counsel may use her questions regarding answers to interrogatories in an attempt to pin down and limit the opinions you will be giving at trial.

Example 5.16

Q: Let me direct your attention to what we've marked as Exhibit No. 1. These are expert answers to interrogatories. I direct your attention to the page which has your name on it. (Pause.) Have you read that document before today?

A: No.

Q: Are those the opinions that you're going to render at trial?

> **Counsel:** Objection in that that's a summary prepared by counsel. If you can answer the question.

A: I need some time to review this document. I think that the elements included here are well...reasonably my own viewpoint.

Q: Are there any other areas that you're going to render opinions about that are not listed on this document?

A: I have no preconception of the opinions that will be rendered at trial...I will try...and respond to the questions that are asked of me to the best of my ability.

Q: So are you saying that this does not include all the areas that you anticipate testifying on because you don't know what you're going to testify on? Is that right?

A: I anticipate to respond honestly to the questions asked of me.

Q: I wasn't questioning your integrity or your honesty. What I was asking you about was whether or not there are other areas you are going to render opinions on that are not listed here on Exhibit No. 1.

A: I have not reviewed that in detail, but I think the testimony will be referenced to the elements of this case in front of us. To the extent that that includes that, that's all I anticipate testifying about.

Lesson: The expert witness has made some important concessions. In this deposition, counsel then went on to question the expert witness about the lengthy and detailed answers to interrogatories concerning what he was going to testify to at trial. Counsel repeatedly asked the question, "Is that your opinion and is that what you will be testifying to?" The expert witness was at a serious disadvantage due to the fact that counsel had not reviewed these answers with him before they were filed and immediately prior to the deposition. The expert made the situation worse by not taking the time during the deposition to review carefully and fully all of the answers *before* he started to give his crucial opinion testimony.

Example 5.17

Q: As I understand it, you will be testifying that Ms. Colombaro is unable to work due to her herniated disk, is that correct, Doctor?

A: Yes.

Q: Are there any other opinions that you will be offering in this case, Doctor?

A: Yes.

Q: What other opinions will you be offering, Doctor?

A: Well, first that her herniated disk was a result of her lifting at work on 1/3/98 and secondly that she has developed a mild to moderate depression as a result of her back injury.

Q: So, we've got all of your opinions set forth in that report and you don't intend to prepare any more reports, correct?

A: Not at this point.

Lesson: You need to be prepared for the open-ended "Will you be offering any other opinions?" question. If

you answer such a question with an absolute "No,"
presenting additional opinions at trial may be
problematic. The "Not at this point" answer was a
good one because it left the door open for additional
opinions to be presented later.

5.4 Factual Basis of an Opinion

Your opinion is only as good as the factual assumptions
upon which it is based. You can expect to be
questioned closely regarding the facts you assumed and
the reports, tests, and other evidence you relied upon in
forming your opinion. Counsel may use this
information to help her dispute these facts at trial. If
she can do so successfully, your opinion may be
invalidated. Counsel may also attempt to alter the facts
and ask you hypothetical questions based on a different
fact pattern. To excel during your deposition, you need
to handle questions regarding the factual basis of your
opinion properly. The authors recommend the
following.

1. Master the facts of the case as part of your
    preparation for the deposition. (See pages
    47-49 on mastering the facts.)
2. Don't be evasive. Where appropriate,
    readily admit that *if* you were given false or
    inaccurate information, your opinion might
    be wrong. The truth of the facts underlying
    your opinion is something the attorneys will
    fight about at trial. It's their problem, not
    yours. All you should do is make sure your
    opinion is based upon the best information
    available to you and that this information is
    reasonably reliable.

3. Be prepared for hypotheticals and "Would it change your opinion if I told you that..." questions. These questions will most likely be based upon the opposing side's theory of the case. You should get this theory from the counsel that retained you during your pre-deposition conference. For example, if their theory is that your patient was "faking it," you might expect the following hypothetical: "Doctor, let's assume for the time being that the plaintiff lied to you when she told you she had discomfort in her back. Would that change your opinion?" You need to be prepared for this kind of hypothetical and will need to answer it as well as possible, giving ground where appropriate.

Example 5.18
Q: What is the basis of your opinion that she had a depressive reaction prior to the date of the accident, June 2, 1986?
A: I based my opinion on her symptoms and the records.
Q: Doctor, prior to June 2, 1986, Ms. Allen didn't have a loss of energy, did she?
A: Not that I know of.
Q: Doctor, prior to June 2, 1986, she wasn't tearful, was she?
A: Not that I know of.
Q: Prior to June 2, 1986, she wasn't irritable, was she?
A: Not that I know of.
Q: Prior to June 2, 1986, she wasn't emotionally labile, was she?
A: Not that I know of.

Q: Prior to June 2, 1986, she didn't evidence sleep problems, did she?
A: Not that I know of.
Q: Prior to June 2, 1986, she didn't feel less of a person, did she?
A: Not that I know of.
Q: Prior to June 2, 1986, she didn't see herself as damaged, did she?
A: Not that I know of.
Q: Prior to June 2, 1986, she did not describe herself as not being herself, did she?
A: Not that I know of.
Q: You're not aware of her having any difficulty concentrating prior to June 2, 1986, are you?
A: I'm not aware of it.
Q: In fact, the medical records don't contain any reference to her having difficulty concentrating prior to June 2, 1986; do they?
A: I believe that's true.
Q: The medical records don't indicate, prior to June 2, 1986, that she was emotionally labile, do they?
A: That's my understanding.
Q: The medical records prior to June 2, 1986, don't evidence any irritability on her part, do they?
A: Not that I am aware of.
Q: Prior to June 2, 1986, she wasn't easily distracted, was she?
A: Not that I'm aware of.
Q: There's nothing in the medical records before June 2, 1986, indicating that she was easily distracted; correct?
A: That is correct.
Q: Prior to June 2, 1986, she didn't have any impaired social relations, did she?
A: Not that I'm aware of.

Q: Prior to June 2, 1986, there's no evidence that she had the feeling of vulnerability; correct?
A: Not that I'm aware of.
Q: Prior to June 2, 1986, there's no evidence that she had a concern over her bodily functions?
A: Not that I'm aware of.
Q: There's no evidence prior to June 2, 1986, that she had an inability to go on with her life; correct?
A: Not that I'm aware of.
Q: Doctor, in fact, there's no evidence of symptoms or medical records prior to June 2, 1986, that show Ms. Allen being depressed, is there?
A: I don't believe so.

Lesson: Once the expert rendered an opinion that was inconsistent with the facts and records, he was in deep trouble. In the example above, counsel has effectively destroyed the credibility of the expert. Experts should be particularly careful about the assumptions and factual basis upon which they build their opinions. If the building blocks can be made to crumble at deposition, so will the entire testimony of the expert.

Example 5.19
Q: You're saying, nowhere in the medical record indicates that she lost consciousness?
A: That the Massachusetts General report was that she did not experience loss of consciousness.
Q: That's your recollection of the Mass. General Hospital report?
A: Correct.
Q: And if it did indicate a reported loss of consciousness, would that change your opinion?

A: If the Massachusetts General Hospital report was that she had experienced some loss of consciousness, then I would be influenced by that, yes.

Q: If eyewitnesses testified that she lost consciousness after this fall, would that change your opinion?

A: Well, I don't know that it would change my opinion, but it's something I would take into account.

Q: If eyewitness testified that she lost consciousness, would that affect your opinion?

A: Well, I would have to, you know, hear what they had to say and all. The—what I have at this point is that Mrs. Dawson thinks that she might have experienced a few seconds of unconsciousness and the medical reports say no loss of consciousness, or the other doctor said that she was not knocked out.

Q: If there was evidence of loss of consciousness, would you consider changing your opinion?

A: If there was evidence that she had lost consciousness, then I would be inclined to think that she had lost consciousness.

Q: Would you consider changing your opinion?

A: Yes, I would.

Lesson: The opinion of the expert in this example is only as good as the factual assumption upon which it is based (that there was no loss of consciousness). The attorney is attempting to attack the opinion by disproving the opinion's factual assumption. The expert has done a good job in admitting that his opinion may change if the facts were different. The expert realizes that the dispute about the underlying facts is to a large extent the attorneys' problem, not his.

METHODOLOGY

You can expect to be questioned closely regarding the methods you used to determine the facts upon which you based your opinions. If counsel can attack the methodology you used to gather facts and evidence, he can ultimately challenge the validity of your opinion and may be able to exclude it from evidence.[3] You need to be prepared to answer challenges to your fact gathering. More importantly, you need to use a reliable and proven methodology that will withstand close questioning by counsel at deposition and trial.

Example 5.20

Q: Do you know the source of that hand drawing?

A: It was produced through Mr. Brown. Whether he actually made the drawing or not, I don't recall at this point.

Q: Do you know whether that drawing was produced by an engineer?

A: I have assumed that it was not.

Q: So in order to make the conclusion that your exemplar wrench deformed to a curve which you described as being very similar to that of the subject wrench, you relied on a hand drawing that was prepared by a layman and a snapshot photograph of the wrench, is that correct to say?

A: Those are the two things I relied on. The photograph that I have is enlarged to eight by ten and there are various photographs of that particular wrench.

Q: Did you use any photometric process to determine the exact curve of the subject wrench?

A: No.

---

[3] See *Daubert v. Merrell Dow Pharmaceuticals, Inc.*, 113 S.Ct. 2786 (1993).

Q: You kind of did that by eyeballing, is that fair to say?

A: That is the term.

Lesson: This was an effective assault on the methods relied upon to form the expert's opinion. The expert would have been wise to rely upon methods that the jury would see as more reliable.

Your deposition may be taken for the specific purpose of determining whether it meets the admissibility standards set forth in *Daubert, Joiner, Kumho Tire,* and subsequent cases. *Daubert* set forth a nonexclusive checklist for trial courts (i.e., trial judges) to use in assessing the reliability of scientific expert testimony. The specific factors explicated by the *Daubert* court are: (1) whether the expert's technique or theory can be or has been tested; that is, whether the expert's theory can be challenged in some objective sense, or whether it is instead simply a subjective, conclusory approach that cannot reasonably be assessed for reliability; (2) whether the technique or theory has been subject to peer review and publication; (3) the known or potential rate of error of the technique or theory when applied; (4) the existence and maintenance of standards and controls; and (5) the degree to which the technique or theory has been generally accepted in the scientific community.

Courts both before and after *Daubert* have found other factors relevant in determining whether expert testimony is sufficiently reliable to be considered by the trier of fact. These factors include the following.

1. Whether experts are "proposing to testify about matters growing naturally and directly

out of research they have conducted independent of the litigation, or whether they have developed their opinions expressly for purposes of testifying." [See *Daubert v. Merrell Dow Pharmaceuticals, Inc.*, F.3d 1311, 1317 (9th Cir. 1995).]

2. Whether the expert has unjustifiably extrapolated from an accepted premise to an unfounded conclusion. [See *General Elec. Co. v. Joiner*, 118 (S.Ct. 512, 519, 1997). This decision notes that in some cases a trial court "may conclude that there is simply too great an analytical gap between the data and the opinion proffered."]

3. Whether the expert has accounted for obvious alternative explanations adequately. [See *Claar v. Burlington N.R.R..*, 29 F.3d 499 (9th Cir. 1994). Here testimony is excluded where the expert failed to consider other obvious causes for the plaintiff's condition. Compare *Ambrosini v. Labarraque*, 101 F.3d 129 (D.C.Cir. 1996). This decision holds that the possibility of some uneliminated causes presents a question of weight, so long as the most obvious causes have been considered and reasonably ruled out by the expert.]

4. Whether the expert "is being as careful as he would be in his regular professional work outside his paid litigation consulting." [See *Sheehan v. Daily Racing Form, Inc.*, 104 F.3d 940, 942 (7th Cir. 1997). See also *Braun v. Lorillard Inc.*, 84 F.3d 230, 234 (7th Cir. 1996). *Daubert* requires the trial court to assure itself that the expert "adheres to the same standards of intellectual rigor

that are demanded in his professional
work."]
5. Whether the field of expertise claimed by
the expert is known to reach reliable results.
[See *Sterling v. Velsicol Chem. Corp.*, 855
F.2d 1188 (6th Cir. 1988), where the court
rejects testimony based on "clinical
ecology" as unfounded and unreliable.]

All of these factors remain relevant to the
determination of the reliability of expert testimony.
In the case of *Stasior v. National Railroad
Passenger Corp.*, 19 F.Supp.2d 835 (N.D.Ill. 1998), the
depositions of ergonomists were taken and then tested
in a motion in limine under *Daubert*. The transcript of
a portion of the lengthy deposition of Michael D.
Shinnick, PhD, a highly regarded ergonomist, is
provided in the example that follows.

Example 5.21
Q: Did you quantify the number of key strokes per
minute the reservation sales agents perform at the
Chicago facility?
A: No.
Q: Do you know if Miss Stasior was using this wrist
rest in 1991 and prior to that time?
A: I don't believe she was but I also know they had
different keyboards at that point and I'm aware that
keys would malfunction and I have—it's been reported
to me that the keyboards that they had prior to the ones
they have now were—required more force.
Q: Do you know when those keyboards were used?
A: No.

Q: As you sit here today, Doctor, can you tell me what keyboard Miss Stasior worked on and for what period of time she worked on it?

A: No.

Q: Do you have any idea if that's what the job looked like and how she performed it in 1991 and prior to that time?

A: There was different equipment, but no.

Q: Let me interrupt you for a minute. You say there's different equipment. We might as well cover this while we're sitting here right now. Do you know the dimensions of the different equipment?

A: No.

Q: Do you know the height of the different equipment?

A: No.

Q: Do you know the height of the desk?

A: No.

Q: Do you know the width of the desk?

A: No.

Q: Do you know the height of the different chair?

A: No. They certainly didn't in the video and she said that's been her customary work posture. But prior to '91, no, I don't know.

Q: Do you know if she ever requested any different equipment prior to 1991?

A: No.

Q: Do you feel you have visited the Amtrak reservation sales office for a sufficient length of time in order to render opinions in this case?

A: Yes.

Q: How long was your visit at the Amtrak reservation sales office in January of 1997?

A: Don't know.

Q: Are you aware of any of the personal risk factors that Miss Stasior has which have been identified as having an association with carpal tunnel syndrome?

A: No.

Q: Did you feel it necessary to determine if she had any personal risk factors in arriving at your opinions in this case?

A: No, not once. I looked at her job and her normal working position and the lack of ergonomic training, no.

Q: Did you quantify—and I apologize, I may repeat a little bit here—did you quantify the length of time Miss Stasior would spend with her wrists in a non-neutral position during the day?

A: No.

Q: As you sit here today, do you know for a fact what type of keyboard Miss Stasior was using in 1991 and before?

A: I do not know for a fact.

Q: As you sit here today, do you know for a fact what chair she was using in 1991 and before?

A: It's not relevant.

Q: So, in your opinion her job caused her condition?

A: From a ergonomic perspective, yes.

Q: Tell me the methodology you used to reach that conclusion.

A: Well, I think we went—she was exposed to multiple risk factors.

Q: Which you did not quantify, right?

A: Don't have to.

Q: They're just there?

A: Yah.

Q: No matter what degree, they're there, that's enough.

A: We don't have thresholds.

Q: Do you have any idea what the prevalence rate of carpal tunnel syndrome is with not only the Amtrak—well, I'll limit it to the Chicago office with the reservation sales office.

A: The prevalence with—no, I don't.

Q: Do you have any idea what the prevalence is with the various reservation sales offices around the country for Amtrak?

A: No.

Q: Would that be a significant thing to know in determining whether or not the job caused carpal tunnel syndrome?

A: No.

Q: Is there any way to test your opinion that Miss Stasior's job caused her carpal tunnel?

A: Test it? Well, I think you can validate it by looking at what other industries have done as far as—and compare that to what Amtrak did not do.

Q: Can you tell me if they did provide the information she would not have developed carpal tunnel syndrome?

A: Well, I can tell you—I can say the probability would be reduced.

Q: But you can't tell me how much?

A: No.

Q: Have you in fact tested your hypotheses that Miss Stasior's work contributed to her carpal tunnel syndrome in any way?

A: No.

Lesson: The court rejected the above deposition testimony, finding that it was not admissible. The rationale of the court is instructive.

> The court holds that while Dr. Shinnick is qualified as an expert to render an opinion regarding causation, his actual testimony is not reliable under *Daubert* because he has not subjected his opinions to the scientific method.[12] Essentially, Dr. Shinnick

---

[12] Because the court finds that Dr. Shinnick's testimony is not reliable under *Daubert*, the court does not address whether Dr. Shinnick's testimony satisfies *Daubert's* relevance requirement.

"identified" the existence of risk factors and then concluded that these risk factors contributed to Stasior's CTS without performing any scientific tests or comparing the data he collected to scientific or epidemiological studies conducted by other ergonomists. Dr. Shinnick never observed the workstation Stasior used in 1991 and before, and he made no attempt to measure the awkward posture and repetition which are allegedly present at Stasior's current workstation in order to extrapolate what her pre-1991 conditions were like. (Shinnick Dep. 27-29, 17-20, 99, 44-45.) Dr. Shinnick simply assumes, without citing any corroborating authority, that because Stasior allegedly was not trained in the proper use of her equipment, the risk factors of awkward posture and repetition must have been present at Stasior's workstation in 1991 and before. (Shinnick Dep. At 21.) While Dr. Shinnick performed functional capacity and grip tests on Stasior, he does not cite any peer-reviewed scientific or epidemiological studies tying the results of his tests to the conclusion that awkward posture and repetition contributed to Stasior's CTS and tendonitis. The court also notes that Dr. Herrin did not base his proffered testimony on research he conducted independent of this litigation, but rather formulated his opinion expressly for the purpose of testifying. (Shinnick Dep. At 42-44.)

Dr. Shinnick defends his "methodology" by stating that any prudent employer does not care about quantifying a risk factor but rather about minimizing any risk factors that exist. (Shinnick Dep. At 99-100.) The court notes that this is a sensible assumption for an ergonomist whose job is to minimize the possibility of developing CTDs in a work environment. However, the analysis required to prospectively minimize the risk factors for CTDs is substantially different from the analysis required to determine specific causes of injuries that have already occurred. *Bennett,* 931 F.Supp. at 493. Because the allocation of legal and possibly substantial financial responsibility is at issue in this case, Dr. Shinnick must base his causation opinions on scientifically reliable methodologies. *Id.* at 493-494. Because Dr. Shinnick does not test his causation opinion in accordance with the scientific method, the court holds that his testimony is not reliable under *Daubert* and therefore is inadmissible.

...The court also holds that Dr. Shinnick's opinion as to forseeability is not reliable under *Daubert*. While Dr. Shinnick states "Amtrak could have known and should have known that the duties routinely performed by Mrs. Stasior placed her in danger of developing cumulative trauma injuries," (Shinnick Report at 4), he is unable to cite any studies from 1991 or before showing that the degree of posture, repetition and force at Amtrak's Chicago RSO was ergonomically unsafe. Therefore, it would be unreasonable to expect Amtrak to have foreseen that the workstation it provided Stasior would have contributed to her CTS and chronic tendonitis.

Because Dr. Shinnick's testimony is not reliable under *Daubert* and therefore inadmissible under Rule 702, the court grants Amtrak's Motion to Bar Testimony of Michael Shinnick.[4]

EQUIPMENT AND TESTING

Counsel who can show that the expert was sloppy in his or her use of equipment and testing can undermine the expert's credibility and cast substantial doubt on his or her results and opinion. Remember, your opinion is

---

[4] *Stasior v. National Railroad Passenger Corp.,* 19 F.Supp.2d 835, 852-853 (N.D. Ill. 1998).

only as good as the facts, equipment, and tests upon which it is based.

Example 5.22

Q: How did you reach your conclusions on the exemplar fender?

A: I made certain measurements of features on the fenders that remained constant both in the photographs and in the flesh and then scaled those down to locate the location of the gouges.

Q: How did you do that?

A: Tape measure and the photographs.

Q: You just took the photographs and—you know, what type of ruler did you use?

A: Steel tape measure, a little six-inch rule, something like that.

Q: Do you know what you used?

A: I typically use a six-inch ruler. I may have used a—

Q: What was the degree of resolution on the measuring instrument used? You mean a 16th of an inch?

A: Hundredths of an inch, something like that.

Q: Excuse me?

A: Hundredths of an inch, something like that.

Q: Was it hundredths of an inch?

A: I would have been using a ruler and a caliper both to do that.

Q: You did use a caliper?

A: Yes.

Q: What type of ruler did you use? I want to know the resolution on it. Was it hundredths of an inch?

A: I don't remember. Caliper would go down to well less than that, but I don't remember what the ruler uses.

Q: So you don't know what the resolution was on the ruler that you used?

A: I don't know which ruler I used, offhand.

Q: Is it one you took with you?

A: No. I did this in the laboratory.

Q: Here in Troy, Michigan?

A: Yes.

Q: And you have no way of going back and determining what ruler you used for your scaling?

A: Probably not. I mean, I've got half a dozen different types of measuring things in my desk.

Q: And you didn't detail the measurements that you took off the photographs of the accident vehicle either, did you...?

Lesson: The expert in the above example may have done nothing wrong, but his "I don't remember" and "I don't know" replies do not instill confidence in him or in his opinion.

THOROUGHNESS

If counsel can imply that you were not thorough, she can challenge the factual foundation of your opinion. If the factual foundation of your opinion is challenged successfully, your opinion may be easily discredited. Counsel will sometimes ask questions that at first sound innocuous, but that get to the thoroughness of your methods.

Example 5.23

Q: Have you been to the accident site in this case?

A: No.

Q: Do you have any desire to go?

A: No.

Q: As far as you know, you're not going to go?

A: That's correct.

Lesson: Counsel has quickly established at deposition that the expert has not, will not, and did not even have a desire to visit the accident scene. At trial, this may be portrayed by counsel as a lack of thoroughness on the part of the expert witness.

5.5 Summary Questions

You should pay particular attention to counsel at deposition when he or she attempts to summarize your entire testimony in one question, answer, or statement. Frequently, counsel will attempt to trick the expert into making an error or may intentionally or unintentionally mischaracterize the prior testimony. When confronted with questions of this type, it is acceptable to respond, "I don't agree with your characterizations" if you don't agree with them. It is also important that you have counsel clarify any broad or ambiguous terms that the jury can interpret differently later on.

Example 5.24

Q: You have just been asked a series of questions to offer an opinion about the causal relation between Mr. Lynch's employment and his occupational disease. Are you now telling the jury that, upon my questioning, that you no longer have an opinion as to the cause of this disease?

A: I would state that I have not testified as to what the cause of Mr. Lynch's carpal tunnel syndrome or cumulative trauma disorder is.

Q: Is that because you don't know?

A: In this case, I don't know.

> **Counsel:** I will therefore move to have the doctor's entire direct examination testimony stricken from the record as he has just stated

that he does not know the cause and therefore his opinion as stated earlier has absolutely no merit and is without any basis.

Lesson: Counsel in the above videotaped deposition was able to call into serious question the entire testimony of the expert as a result of the expert's reply to one summary question. You need to be especially careful when answering these broad "soundbite" type of questions.

5.6 Bias

Expert witnesses are routinely questioned during deposition by counsel to determine if they have any bias that may affect their credibility. The general evidentiary rule is that this line of inquiry is permitted because matters that affect bias are relevant to a crucial issue in the case—your credibility as a witness. Counsel is given great leeway to discover any interest, bias, or motive for testimony that would serve to discredit the expert's testimony.

> An honest independent expert who would never dream of giving false testimony under any circumstances may nevertheless end up inadvertently doing just that. His subconscious partiality for the side which has sought his services may color his evaluation of the facts of the case and his opinions.[5]

---

[5] Robert C. Habush, *Art of Advocacy: Cross-Exam of Non-Medical Experts* (New York, NY: Matthew Bender, 1998) Sec. 300 (2).

There are three things that you can do to deal properly with questioning regarding your possible biases.

1. Tell the truth and "call them as you see them." This policy will enable you to testify with confidence supported by the courage of your convictions.
2. State that your opinion is independent and unbiased.

    > The witness should make it clear, to the extent possible, that the engagement began without preconceptions concerning any issue and without any predisposition in favor of or opposed to any party or counsel. The expert was not told what opinion to come to but was asked to render an honest opinion and did so.[6]

3. Try not to testify exclusively for only one side in cases. This may not be achieved easily because counsel and industry may peg you or refuse to use you if you testify for the other side.

The standard areas of bias that experts are challenged on during their depositions are covered in the following sections.

IMPARTIALITY

Counsel can damage the credibility of the expert by showing that the expert is not being impartial. This may be done by showing that the expert only testifies

---

[6] Gregory P. Joseph, *ALI-ABA's Practice Checklist Manual on Taking Depositions* (Philadelphia, PA: American Law Institute, 1995) 89.

for one side. For example, she only testifies for plaintiffs. Counsel is trying to show that the expert wouldn't want to put future referrals at risk by proffering testimony that her client wouldn't like. To excel during depositions, you will need to be able to handle this line of questioning. As always, you want to answer the questions simply and directly. If you try to cover up your propensities to testify for one side, these propensities will only be emphasized to the jury. You will also want to clarify in advance a rationale for why you usually testify for one side. For example, you may state that as an orthopedic surgeon you usually testify on behalf of plaintiffs because they are also patients who you have treated and you are the physician most familiar with their cases.

Example 5.25
Q: You have testified in other workers' compensation cases also on behalf of the employer?
A: Yes, I have.
Q: Do you recall each and every instance of testimony that you gave?
A: No, I do not.
Q: Is it true that in workers' compensation cases you testify mostly on behalf of employers?
A: I would state that's a fair statement; yes.

Lesson: The expert was straightforward and did not try to mislead the jury about his prior testimony. This ended this inquiry and counsel then went on to inquire about the expert's opinion.

Example 5.26

Q: Is it true that in workers' compensation cases you testify mostly on behalf of employers?

A: No; employers and for employees as well.

Q: Have you ever testified that an injured worker contracted carpal tunnel syndrome as the result of work?

A: Yes, I have.

Q: What was the name of the person that you testified on behalf of?

A: I can't—I cannot—obviously, patient confidentiality would restrict me from divulging—

Q: Don't give me that patient confidentiality, Doctor. I asked you if you testified on behalf of someone. You know very well there's no—

A: Testified—

Q: —patient confidentiality. I'm asking you—

A: Okay.

Q: —did you ever testify?

A: You define for me what testify means.

Q: Like here in open court, in a deposition or in court, did you ever give a deposition—

A: I've indicated in—I've indicated in—

Q: —on behalf of an injured worker?

A: —medical records that, and I've written letters to the effect that I felt an individual had developed carpal tunnel syndrome.

Q: So I can break your answer down, sir. The answer is, you cannot recall any instances where you testified on behalf of an injured worker that they contracted carpal tunnel at work, correct? Testified!

A: Define testified, please?

Q: Deposition or trial.

A: As I indicated, I cannot recall any specific incident that I've testified in court or on deposition, and my safe assumption is that it never had to go that far.

Lesson: The expert in this case attempted to make his testimony sound more impartial than it actually might have been. Keep in mind that this was a videotape deposition intended to be used in lieu of live testimony at trial. The expert would probably have been better served by answering the first question with a simple yes. His evasiveness makes him look like he is an advocate and has something to hide. This encourages counsel to emphasize the point instead of moving on. This is far more damaging to his credibility than would have been an admission that he testifies mostly for employers.

Example 5.27
Q: Well, in your report you state that to a reasonable— I'm going to paraphrase it—to a reasonable degree of certainty Mrs. Sanford's job—
A: What page are you on?
Q: Why don't I just go ahead and get it for you so I can actually not paraphrase it? Page 4, second paragraph, what looks like about the third full sentence: "Within a reasonable ergonomic certainly a causal relationship exists between Mrs. Sanford's job duties and damage to the carpal tunnels." Other than this case have you ever offered such an opinion?
A: Sure.
Q: Have you ever in a case in which you were retained to examine the workplace and possibly offer opinions in a carpal tunnel case, have you ever had a contrary opinion?
A: No. I've had different opinions but no, I haven't.
Q: In your opinion the workplace has always caused the carpal tunnel syndrome?
A: Yes, but that's—yes, that's what I've found.

Lesson: If you can be portrayed as always arriving at the same opinion, your impartiality and credibility may be called into question.

INFLEXIBILITY

If counsel can show during the deposition that you are inflexible (nothing would change your opinion), this is another indication of potential bias. If the underlying factual assumptions are changed and you still refuse to admit you may have to change your opinion, your credibility will come into question. To refute these kinds of attacks on your credibility, you should demonstrate your open-mindedness. This will go a long way in showing a lack of bias.

Example 5.28
Q: If you were to learn that Todd was different after the crash, that would change your opinion, wouldn't it?
A: If I had information indicating that, I would consider it.
Q: If you were to learn that after the car crash, Todd Able began to exhibit signs and symptoms that are the diagnostic of post-traumatic stress disorder, would you be willing to change your opinion?
A: Possibly. I will reiterate that Mr. Able made it very clear to me that he had these classic symptoms from 1973 onward and indicated to me that they were unchanged in their intensity or frequency subsequent to the motor vehicle accident in 1993.
Q: If you were to learn that Mr. Able was incorrect, or if your notation of his statements was incorrect, you would be willing to change your opinion, wouldn't you?
A: The notation of my—of his statements in my records are not incorrect. These are what he told me. If

I learned that there was information indicating that his recollection of that was incorrect, I would consider it. I would not automatically change my opinion since it's after the fact.

Lesson: The expert psychologist demonstrated his willingness to consider new evidence and possibly changing his opinion without actually changing his opinion. He handled these questions well.

PERSONAL/SOCIAL RELATIONSHIP WITH PARTY/ATTORNEY

Another way to show your potential bias is to establish that you have a personal/social relationship with a party or your retaining attorney. The way to handle these questions is honestly and directly. Remember that your own evasiveness can be more damaging to your credibility than whatever point counsel is trying to make. However, be careful that you do not agree with an attempt by counsel to mischaracterize your relationship. For example, if the party is an "acquaintance," don't agree with counsel's assertion that she is a "close friend."

Example 5.29
Q: Are you a close personal friend of Attorney Burns?
A: I am a friend.
Q: Have you been to his home?
A: Yes.
Q: Have you been to his condominium in Vail?
A: Yes.
Q: Did you ski together?
A: Yes.
Q: Do you play racquetball together?
A: Yes.

Q: Are your spouse and his wife friendly?
A: Yes.
Q: How often do you see him socially?
A: Once or twice a week.
Q: Are you a close personal friend of Attorney Burns?
A: Yes—I guess I am.

Lesson: If you disagree with counsel's characterization of your relationship with a party or attorney, you will need to prepare yourself to answer these types of questions.

PROFESSIONAL WITNESS

Counsel may try to portray you as a *professional witness.* A professional witness is a witness who testifies frequently and derives a large percentage of his or her income from forensic work. Counsel is trying to show that such a witness is biased by being consciously or unconsciously hesitant to jeopardize his livelihood by saying something that would hurt the party that retained him. The expert witness that can be portrayed as a *hired gun* due to the frequency with which he or she testifies can quickly be made to lose credibility.

Example 5.30
Q: Doctor, you are an experienced expert witness, are you not?
A: It depends on what you mean by experienced.
Q: You testify quite frequently, don't you?
A: Again, Counselor, it depends on what you mean by frequently.
Q: How many times have you testified in deposition in Massachusetts?
A: 60-80 times.

Q: In addition to depositions you testified daily when you were a court clinic director.

A: That is correct.

Q: What superior courts have you testified in in Massachusetts?

A: Suffolk, Middlesex, Essex, Hampden, Worcester, I believe, Plymouth, Barnstable, Bristol. I think that's about it.

Q: Would you agree that you are an experienced expert witness?

A: It all depends on how you define experienced.

Lesson: Counsel has scored two major points with this witness. First, the doctor is clearly an experienced expert witness. Secondly, she is not forthcoming with any information. Both points will tend to make the jury or fact finder discredit her testimony. As a practical matter, the doctor would have been better off to admit that she was an experienced expert witness.

ADVOCATE

Your role as an expert is to state opinions. Your role is not to be an advocate for one side or the other. That's the attorney's role. If you start to sound or act like an advocate, counsel can paint you as biased and you will lose credibility with the fact finder.

Example 5.31

Q: Your report is fairly detailed, it's an eight-page report to Mr. Benner?

A: That's correct.

Q: Now, on page 3 of your report to Mr. Benner, you state—I'll let you find it.

A: Yes.

Q: Quote, "That although sufficient witnesses have been present, they may not be unbiased witnesses in this particular accident."

A: That's what I stated.

Q: Why did you feel this was important to include in your independent medical report?

A: Mr. Rowe himself quoted that he had 30 witnesses or something so that it was witnessed that he had fallen. But I would challenge you to find one independent or one that would not be his co-worker, friend with the same causes involved. So, yes, you have witnesses; and, yes, witnesses' recollections may or may not be shaded by whatever other circumstances go on, so I felt that they would be witnesses but the direct testimony you're going to get out of them may or may not be useful or entirely reflective of the situation.

Q: And why is it your function as the independent medical evaluator in this case to point that out to Mr. Benner? That's what I'm trying to understand.

A: I'm not sure if it's my function to point that out. It might be my function to try to figure out why there are lots of complaints and lots of treatment and there were none before. And I see lots of secondary factors involved that would be probably more explained—more clearly explanatory of his clinical course than any medical issues involved.

Q: Well, right now we're talking about the witnesses that you're saying are biased in this particular case. Have you reviewed any of the witness statements in the case?

A: I'm not saying they're biased. I'm just commenting that they are probably not unbiased, and I have not reviewed any witness testimony here.

Q: So you really don't have any idea because you don't know what they said?

A: Don't have any idea, just had a feeling that they may not be as unbiased as one would like it to be.

Lesson: The physician has left his role as an independent medical evaluator and unbiased expert and has become part of the litigation team for the defense. As a result, it is likely that he will lose credibility.

FEES AND COMPENSATION

The fact that you are being paid for your time (remember always that you are never paid for your testimony, only for your time) is relevant to a possible bias toward the party who retained you. Questions about your expert witness fees and compensation are legitimate and relevant. The fact that you are being paid a fee is not something you should be ashamed of because as a professional your time is valuable. Keep in mind also that the experts retained by the opposing side will also be charging a fee for their time, so counsel can only make so much of trying to show bias through your fee.

When questioning an expert about fees, counsel frequently attempts to get the expert to be defensive and, if possible, evasive. If the jury or fact finder gets the impression that the expert is trying to hide something, is doing something he or she is ashamed of, or is trying to conceal something, the honesty and integrity of the witness come into question quickly. In legal parlance, this is known as using a *red-herring* or making something out of nothing. As an expert, you can protect yourself from such legal tactics by answering questions about your fees in a straight-forward manner.

The fee that you charge can be very high and still not damage your credibility. The key is to be able to justify the fee that you charge. For example, if you are a plastic surgeon charging $600.00/hour for your time, you could justify this fee by pointing out the surgical revenue you are foregoing by testifying and how your overhead costs remain extensive while you testify.

Example 5.32
Q: Okay. How much did you receive in fees for doing your examination and report?
A: I received the usual and customary fee.
Q: And what is that?
A: I am not at liberty to provide that.
Q: Well, sir, you're under oath at testimony here at trial, you're sworn to tell the truth. How much did you get paid for preparing the report and performing the examination?
    Counsel: If you know, go ahead and answer.
A: I would have to go look it up.
Q: Okay. How much are you charging for your time to testify here this morning?
A: Again, charging the usual and customary fee.

Q: Do you keep any records of how much you have made testifying as an expert witness on a yearly basis?
A: No.
Q: Do you have any estimate of what you have made as an expert witness in the last year, in 1996, since we all just finished our income tax returns?
A: No, we haven't. I sent an extension in.
Q: Do you have an estimate of what you made in the last year?
A: I don't.
Q: Do you have an estimate of what percentage of your income is derived from testifying as an expert witness?

A: Yah, I think I could probably give you a guesstimate on that.

Lesson: Note how evasive the experts appear over questions that could have and should have been answered simply and directly. Some experts honestly don't know how much they are billing because someone else in their office takes care of sending out the bills. In order to avoid such exchanges, these experts should find out what their rates and incomes are before they testify at deposition.

Example 5.33
Q: How much money was Packer paid last year by Honda in connection with ATV matters?
A: I don't know.
Q: You have no idea?
A: No.
Q: How much was Packer paid last year by Yamaha in connection with ATV matters?
A: I don't know.
Q: How much did Packer receive last year from Honda as a result of work you did?
A: I don't know.
Q: You don't have any estimate of what your billings were to Honda last year or to lawyers who were representing Honda in litigation matters?
A: No.
Q: What were your billings to Honda for the Wollin case?
A: I don't know what that is....

Lesson: Expert witnesses who can be made to answer, "I don't know" over and over again with regard to their fees or the fees of their company may look uninformed and, in extreme cases, evasive.

Example 5.34

Q: Have you billed Mr. Pirok yet for your time?

A: Yes.

Q: How much time did you bill him for?

A: I have no idea.

> **Counsel:** Ed, I'd like a copy of that bill if I could.
>
> **Attorney:** Yah, maybe I can have it faxed over to you.
>
> **Counsel:** You don't have to do it right now.
>
> **Attorney:** Might as well, otherwise it will get delayed and I can just have it faxed over.

Q: How much time did you spend preparing your opinions and your report?

A: If my invoice will be faxed over here it will have a chronological statement, and we can look at that.

Q: We'll go back to that. It's coming over.

> **Attorney:** My secretary is out to lunch—I guess since it's Secretaries' Day—and she's going to call here. I already left a message to fax the stuff, but I don't know if she's got your fax number and everything, so she'll give us a call and we'll get it.

A: If that occurs, I can respond specifically from that; if it doesn't, then I'll give you a guesstimate.

Lesson: Your bills to the attorney who retained you are a legitimate area of inquiry. You should be prepared to be questioned closely about the content of these bills.

Example 5.35

Q: How much do you make an hour in connection with your litigation-related work?

A: All my time is billed by the company at the same rate, which is $450 an hour currently.

Q: Okay, and I know you've been asked these questions a lot in connection with litigation, and I've seen some printouts that you've done that have numbers on them and the whole bit. As you sit here today, do you have an estimate of how much your company's been paid by Honda in connection with ATV-related cases—

A: For all—

Q: —and work?

A: It's certainly more than two million dollars. Maybe up to three million now. Something in—around there. I don't know exactly.

Q: I take it you hope to continue to testify on behalf of Honda in the future—in these type of cases?

A: Absolutely.

Lesson: The argument of bias is especially strong if counsel can show that the expert testifies a lot for a single client or industry. The argument that is made to the jury is, "Now, Mr. Expert wouldn't want to say or do anything that will jeopardize his little $3,000,000 business, would he?" The expert in this case did a good job of not being evasive when answering these questions. Had he been evasive, it only would have made a bad situation worse.

FINANCIAL INTEREST IN THE CASE

Counsel may try to show that an expert stands to gain in the future from the outcome of the case. This gain may be the likelihood of future work as an expert witness. Counsel who can imply that an expert has a financial interest in the outcome seriously undermines the credibility of the expert.

Example 5.36

Q: All right. Doctor, this procedure that you recommended that Miss Duff have with respect to her lower back, that's a surgical procedure, right?

A: Yes.

Q: Okay. And you were going to be the one that was going to perform that procedure, right?

A: If she wanted me to.

Q: Okay. And you weren't going to perform that surgery for free, were you, sir?

A: No.

Q: All right. You charge for your time as a surgeon, correct?

A: That's correct.

Q: Okay. What fee do you charge for performing the surgeries that you told counsel about that you do about five or ten times or eight to ten times a month?

A: That would depend on what the surgery was.

Q: All right. Let's talk about the garden-variety common laminectomy that you would perform to correct herniated disc at the L4-5 level. What is your fee for doing that procedure, sir?

A: I do not know.

Q: You do not know?

A: No, sir.

Q: Okay. How long have you been practicing as a surgeon, sir?

A: Working 10 years.

Q: All right. And how many surgeries have you performed over the years?

A: Thousands.

Q: All right. And you have no memory or knowledge of what you charge as a surgeon to perform a lumbar laminectomy at the L4-5 level?

A: No, sir.

Lesson: Note how arrogant and foolish the expert sounds when he says he does not know how much he charges for surgery. This expert's credibility was further undermined because he would make money from the surgery he recommended.

PROFESSIONAL DISCIPLINE

The professional discipline tactic is one frequently employed by counsel to back the expert witness into an untenable position. When using this tactic, counsel will attempt to turn a disagreement between experts into a flagrant ethical violation. To defeat this tactic, you need to be extremely careful when responding to questions about another expert's actions. Consider the following example.

Example 5.37

Q: And Dr. Smedling found that this person, Terry Fillus had a psychiatric disorder, correct?

A: Yes.

Q: And Dr. Smedling offered the opinion that the psychiatric disorder was a result of the occupational asthma?

A: Yes.

Q: You would also agree with me that Dr. Dowd found the presence of psychiatric disorder in Terry Fillus?

A: Yes.

Q: So doctor, we're clear, Terry Fillus was able to fool two other doctors, right?

A: I don't know if it was fooling.

Q: She wasn't able to fool you, was she?

A: I don't know.

Q: Well, doctor, here's this lady with a ninth grade education and low to normal intelligence and appears that she was able to convince a psychiatrist and a psychologist that she has a psychiatric condition. What happened?

A: What happened? Well, there's a number of things that, that happened. Dr. Smedling relies in part on the psychological test and does not go through criteria for DSM-IV.

Q: So Dr. Smedling didn't do it right, that's why he's wrong, correct?

A: He didn't do it the way to evolve to a DSM-IV diagnosis.

Q: So he misdiagnosed Terry Fillus' condition?

A: I guess so.

Q: Were you shown the treatment notes by Dr. Smedling?

A: No.

Q: Do you know that he's treated her?

A: Yes.

Q: Do you know that he's treated her for several years?

A: No.

Q: Did you know that he's seen her on multiple occasions?

A: Yes.

Q: So he's treating her essentially for a condition that doesn't exist, correct?

A: I don't know.

Q: Well, you say it doesn't exist.

A: I, I don't know what he's treating her for.

Q: Well, if he's treating her for depression or post-traumatic stress disorder, he would be treating her for a condition that doesn't exist?

A: At the—right, at the time that I saw her, right.

Q: Now that you know this information, are you going to turn him into the state licensing board?

A: No.

Q: So you're going to let a doctor go ahead and treat a person for a condition that's not there?

A: Right. Okay. So am I going to turn him into the board? No.

Q: And Dr. Dowd made a misdiagnosis as well, correct?

A: It seems that way.

Q: Are you going to turn him in?

A: No.

Q: So you think it's okay for a doctor to blow the diagnosis and then still get to go out in the world and treat people and not be called to task for it?

A: Yes.

Lesson: The doctor has been forced to answer with a reply that may be unacceptable to him and the jury. He should have been more artful in his criticism of his colleague's methods and actions.

5.7 Mischaracterization of Testimony

You need to be very aware of any attempts by counsel to characterize or mischaracterize your testimony. When employing this tactic, counsel is trying in essence to give testimony herself and simply have you agree with it. To excel during depositions, you need to remember to be very careful before agreeing with one of counsel's characterizations. This is especially true if the characterization is broad or could be ambiguous. When confronted with a characterization that you do not agree with, it is proper to respond that you don't agree with the characterization.

Example 5.38
Q: Wouldn't someone with mechanical aptitude be most likely to.... Given a choice...to have used that screwdriver for the cleaning function?
A: I don't believe there was any testimony that the screwdriver was available at the time of his accident. Clearly, it's in this photograph. We know that certain things have been placed on that fender after the accident so I don't know that in fact that screwdriver was available.
Q: So it's your testimony that you believe that the screwdriver was placed there by someone after the accident occurred?
Objection.
A: That wasn't my testimony.

Lesson: The expert handled this lawyer tactic well. He quickly corrected the "state of the record" and the mischaracterization of his testimony by counsel.

5.8 Catchall Questions

You should be particularly wary of final *wrap up questions* in which counsel asks you if you have anything else to say or add to your testimony. This is a final cast in the fishing expedition. These questions should be answered briefly, but in a way that keeps the door open for future additions. Failure to do so could create problems at trial if you wish to present new or additional information or opinions.

Example 5.39
Q: Do you recall any other information which bears on this case?
A: Not at this time.

Lesson: This is an artful, yet truthful, answer. It is therefore a good answer.

5.9 Authoritative Writings

If you agree that you consider a text authoritative, you may be cross-examined at length from the text. Many experts are thus cautious in agreeing that they consider a text authoritative. An artful way to answer this question might be as follows.

> As with most any published work, the authors or editors state things with which many in the field agree and other things with which they may disagree. Similarly, there may be things with which I agree and other things with which I may disagree. If you would like me to comment on a specific portion of the text, please ask me about that.[7]

Example 5.40
Q: Do you consider the text Smith on Orthopedics to be authoritative?
A: No.

Lesson: Had the expert agreed that the text was "authoritative," she could have been cross-examined at length from it.

---

[7] Rex K. Linder, *Defense Counsel Journal,* Vol. 58, No.2 (April 1991) 177.

5.10 Impeachment

<small>INCONSISTENT PRIOR SWORN TESTIMONY</small>

Your prior sworn testimony in other cases may be used in an attempt to contradict and impeach your deposition testimony. Experienced expert witnesses who have testified frequently may be faced with the daunting task of attempting to explain, justify, recognize, and in some cases, defend their prior sworn testimony. Sophisticated counsel cross-examining the expert at deposition does not warn the expert of this line of attack. Counsel may attempt to "mousetrap" the expert by asking his or her opinion and then bringing up an alleged differing opinion in a prior case. The Rules of Evidence and Procedure permit counsel to use prior sworn testimony in this fashion in an attempt to impeach the expert at deposition.

> Ordinarily, counsel should be permitted to interrogate a party or a witness about apparent inconsistencies between testimony given in court and testimony given on deposition with regard to all matters relevant to the issues at trial. Where credibility is at issue, counsel should be permitted to first question the witness and then confront the witness with a prior inconsistent answer in the witness' deposition; counsel need not give the witness an initial opportunity to admit or deny allegedly inconsistent statements before reading them from the deposition.[8]

When the expert testifies at deposition to a fact or opinion that is inconsistent with his or her sworn statement in a prior case, counsel will first set the trap and then spring it. It is important to note that in today's

---

[8] *Federal Procedure,* Lawyer's Edition (Rochester, NY: Lawyers' Cooperative Publishing, 1994) 686.

information age, your prior deposition and trial testimony transcripts are more and more readily available to attorneys. Furthermore, in federal court, the party that retained you is required to disclose to other parties "a listing of any other cases the witness has testified as an expert at trial or by deposition within the preceding four years."[9]

Example 5.41

Q: Agricultural engineering is a distinct profession, is it not...? The same as mechanical engineering, is that correct?

A: There are degrees listed as agricultural engineers, yes.

Q: Would you agree with the statement that agricultural engineering is a discipline all its own?

A: It has the title of a discipline all its own, yes.

Q: You don't agree with that fully?

A: I don't agree that it's unique unto itself, no.

Q: Didn't you on a prior occasion under oath state that in your opinion that agricultural engineering is a discipline all of its own?

A: I don't recall saying that.

Q: Do you remember giving testimony in the case of *Kelly versus Saskasky?*

A: Saskasky...vaguely.

Q: I have before me a transcript of a deposition that was taken of you in that case in which you were testifying for a manufacturer. I ask you to look at it and tell me if you can identify it as your deposition.

A: It appears to be, yes.

---

[9] Fed. R. Civ. Pro. 26(a)(2)(B).

Q: Would you please read your answer on page six beginning with line 12.

A: Agricultural engineering is a discipline all of its own one portion of which has to do with the design and construction of agricultural equipment and systems used in farming and agricultural food processing and that sort of thing.

Q: Was it true then and is it true today?

A: Yes.

Q: So it would be fair to say, correct to say, that at least as far as the design of agricultural equipment, agricultural engineering is a discipline all its own, is that correct?

A: Yes.

Lesson: Had the expert listened carefully to the question, "Would you agree with the statement that agricultural engineering is a discipline all its own?," he or she could have anticipated an impeachment attempt based on the answer. The expert who tells the truth, prepares by reviewing his or her prior depositions involving similar issues, maintains a consistent opinion, and does not tailor them to meet the needs of his or her client has little to fear from this type of impeachment at deposition.

Example 5.42

Q: Would you agree with the statement, "Keypunching, although it has high repetitiveness, you can punch keys all day long and look at a video display, it doesn't have static loading, it doesn't have force, it doesn't have vibration, it doesn't have all the components of the risk factors which research clearly state compound one another or certainly make the risk much higher"?

A: Yes, I disagree with that. We're talking about frequency.

Q: Do you remember giving trial testimony in the case of *Walker versus Norfolk Western*?

A: Uh-huh. I see you have done your homework.

Q: And do you recall being questioned regarding the NIOSH study of the U.S. West Communication System?

A: Not specifically, no.

Q: Do you disagree with me if it were in the transcript of your testimony?

A: No, probably not. I might have to read the context of it.

Q: Okay. Do you recall being asked these questions and giving these answers:

> "Question: Are NIOSH studies something that you look at and rely on in your work that you do?"

> "Answer: Yes. And in answering your question this is a summary of a study that was done on video display terminals. I am familiar with the fact there was a study that occurred relating to video display operators."

> "Question: All right but they are evaluating so-called cumulative trauma disorders in people who purportedly use repetitive motions in their work, is that right?"

> "Answer: In keypunching."

> "Question: And that's something you would consider to be a repetitive motion?"

> "Answer: Yes, can be."

And then he asked you to turn to page 12 of that report.

> "Would you read the sentence starting with 'overtime?'"

> "Answer: Overtime in the past year had a negative association with increasing shoulder

symptoms. The increasing number of hours spent at a video display terminal or VDT work station per day had a negative association with increasing hand and wrist symptoms."

"Question: You see Dr. Verne Pusz-Anderson's name over there?"

"Answer: It is Putz."

"Question: Is it Putz?"

"Answer: Yah."

"Question: That's a fellow you mentioned a little bit ago on direct examination, wasn't it?"

"Answer: Yes. And what I think is significant is this is about video display terminal keypunch operators, which is not relevant to this case, to Mr. Walker. He didn't punch keys."

"Question: It's what you said is repetitive motion, isn't it?"

"Answer: Punching keys is repetitive motion, yes."

"Question: And that is what you say is one of the risk factors for cumulative trauma disorders?"

Lesson: Your prior testimony is becoming increasingly easy for counsel to obtain. Prior inconsistent testimony can and will come back to haunt you.

PRIOR MISTAKEN DEPOSITION TESTIMONY

You may be confronted with prior mistakes or errors that you have made. The fact that you have made mistakes in the past can affect your credibility. Counsel is seeking to get these mistakes into the record and see how you will react. The best way to react is to admit the mistake if it occurred and not try to cover it up. Juries understand that everyone makes mistakes and may readily forgive this. If you try to cover up your mistake, you may appear evasive or biased. Appearing evasive or biased may be much more difficult for a jury to forgive.

Example 5.43

Q: So your position is that systemic osteoarthritis is not trauma or an activity related disease, correct?

A: That's correct. The pathophysiology is really not known.

Q: In one occasion in the Aggy case you specifically cited an article to me, the *Journal of Bone and Joint Surgery,* 1985, New England edition, which you said supported your position.

A: Right.

Q: And the fact is, there is no such article in the 1985 New England edition of the *Journal of Bone and Joint Surgery;* is that correct?

A: Counselor, I'll make you a deal. You've done this to me three or four times on depositions. I'll have a Med-Line search done at Harper Hospital and find the information that supports my contentions. There are a number of articles that support it. I don't know what article I quoted you there.

Q: I'll read it to you here, doctor.

You stated, quote: "I don't have it with me, but you're welcome to look it up, *Journal of Bone and Joint Surgery,* 1985, New England edition, they did a study on osteoarthritis of the spine, the hands, the extremities, and compared activity levels of individuals, such as coal miners, steel workers, et cetera, versus activity levels of attorneys, barristers and judges and doctors and those that do the heavy activity had the same incidence of those that don't in the same areas of the body with the same amount of complaints of pain."

A: Exactly.

Q: That was your testimony.

A: Exactly.

Q: There's no such article in the *Journal of Bone and Joint Surgery.*

A: There is an article, maybe not be in that magazine, maybe a different year. The article exists. I've quoted it more than once over a period of years. That's not happenstance. That was part of my education. I've read that article. I'll do everything I can to have the powers that be obtain those articles so I can waltz in here every time we have a dep and demonstrate to you that the vast majority of accomplished physicians agree with that contention, because they do.

Q: Based upon your reading of the article you cannot find and may not even exist?

Lesson: The expert has made many mistakes in the above exchange.

1. He was imprecise with the earlier testimony.
2. Despite the fact that the issue keeps coming up, he hasn't bothered to locate the article.
3. He lost his temper.
4. His answers are long and rambling.

The expert's cavalier attitude toward the facts and his prior sworn testimony may seriously affect his credibility with the jury and fact finder. A better way to handle this may have been, "I'm sorry if I made an error reporting the citation. I can try to get you an accurate cite if you like."

YOUR OWN WRITINGS

Counsel at deposition may attempt to impeach you with an article or book that you have written. A comprehensive list of your writings is readily available to counsel through electronic search engines. You should prepare for this type of impeachment by reviewing your published writings. Remember, a competent attorney will do her homework by reviewing your writings. If you don't do the same, you may be trapped by the attorney.

Example 5.44
Q: The normal range for a five-minute Apgar score is considered 7 and above in the predominant medical literature which you've reviewed?
A: Not necessarily.
Q: In your book, *Maternal Infant Medicine, Principles and Practice,* third edition, Wollin and Boyer, 7 and above is set forth as a normal five-minute Apgar, correct?
A: That's correct.
Q: Do you wish to retract the statement you made in your book?
A: No, I will stand by it.

Lesson: Note how quickly counsel was able to cast serious doubt on the expert's "not necessarily" answer. The more accomplished the expert, the more he or she may have written. These experts are often hard pressed to remember everything that they have written if they don't review their pertinent writings. Contradiction by your own writings can be a very effective form of impeachment.

ANOTHER EXPERT'S OPINION

Counsel may use testimony of other experts to impeach, shake, or undermine your deposition testimony.

Example 5.45
Q: In a patient with mild brain injury, the Glasgow Coma Scale must be 13 to 15, correct?
A: No, that's not right.
Q: Dr. Cosgrove, an expert whose deposition we have already taken, has testified on this issue, correct?
A: Yes, I remember seeing his deposition.
Q: He states on page 37 when the patient is evaluated in the emergency room or at the scene, the Glasgow Coma Scale must be 13 to 15 by common definition. As discussed below, only a score of 15 probably represents true mild traumatic brain injury. And you would disagree with that?
A: I would certainly defer, you know, to Dr. Alexander. I'm sure he is more qualified than I am.

Lesson: Counsel used the deposition of another expert to get the witness to change his opinion. Had the expert prepared more thoroughly, the above embarrassment could have been avoided.

CONTRADICTORY FACT TESTIFIED TO BY ANOTHER WITNESS

Counsel may seize on a small and seemingly inconsequential bit of testimony in an attempt to undercut your credibility. The lawyer is trying to show to the jury that if you could be wrong on one fact, you could be wrong on others and your opinion may be suspect. To avoid this type of impeachment, you should thoroughly prepare, concentrate, and testify precisely to the facts of the case.

Example 5.46

Q: Dr. Brandeberry's a family doctor; is that correct?

A: Yes.

Q: Don't you know Dr. Brandeberry?

A: Not personally, sir, no.

Q: Okay. Well, you said he referred the case to you, right?

A: Yes.

Q: Where is the letter of referral?

A: There is no letter of referral.

Q: There is no letter of referral. If I were to tell you, Doctor, that I took Dr. Brandeberry's deposition and he said that he doesn't know you and that he never referred a case to you and didn't refer Mrs. Pollard's case to you, that would be significant, wouldn't it?

A: I wouldn't know how that would happen.

Q: Well, you told the jury that Dr. Brandeberry referred Mrs. Pollard to you?

A: I may have been mistaken.

Lesson: A simple discrepancy can damage an expert's credibility. This expert needed to get his facts straight prior to the deposition.

Chapter 6 Deposition Advice for Expert Witnesses

This chapter contains specific advice to assist you in preparing for your expert deposition. Preparation is essential if you want to excel during your deposition. It may be a good idea to read this section immediately prior to being deposed.

6.1 General Advice

TELL THE TRUTH

The single most important piece of advice for expert witnesses is to tell the truth, simply and directly. This cannot be overemphasized. As an expert witness, you have a legal, moral, and ethical obligation to tell the truth. You are testifying under oath. Experts who tell less than the truth run the risk of criminal prosecution for perjury, civil suits for negligence, and revocation or suspension of their professional licenses. Experts who do not tell the truth are discovered and discredited eventually.

You are allowed, however, to state your truthful answers as artfully as possible. The mark of a great expert witness is one who answers in a way that prevents his opinion from being undermined.

Example 6.1
Q: Is it your testimony that the net present value of this deceased newborn's future earnings is $857,000?
A: Yes, it is.
Q: Mr. Spira, you're really guessing here aren't you? You have no idea what this baby would have earned had she lived?

A: My opinion is based upon demographic and economic statistics. It is a scientifically derived estimate.

Lesson: The expert here could have stated that his "estimate" was a "guess." Both answers are truthful. His response was superior because it was phrased artfully and did not lessen the weight given to his opinion by the jury.

LOCATION

Counsel taking the expert's deposition has the option of conducting the deposition at his or her office, at the office of the expert, or at some neutral location. To save costs, some experts, such as physicians, have traditionally been deposed at their offices. By simply asking the counsel that retained you, you may be able to move the location of the deposition to or away from your office. You need to understand the *advantages* and *disadvantages* of having the deposition taken at your office. These include the following.

1. Less travel involved.
2. More time available for other activities.
3. Feeling more comfortable on "your own turf."
4. Control of logistics: seating, temperature, etc.
5. Staff available to assist.
6. Records available when needed.

While the advantages of being deposed in your own office may seem obvious, the disadvantages are more subtle. These are discussed below.

Disadvantage 1: Interruptions
Interruptions may occur, which can be annoying and
distracting. If you are distracted, you are not likely to
excel during your expert deposition.

Example 6.2
Q: Do you want to answer that phone?
A: No, let it ring. The service will eventually get it.

Lesson: If you are distracted, you will be far more
likely to make a mistake and misspeak.

Disadvantage 2: Unwanted Disclosure of Information
Unwanted disclosure of information may occur
inadvertently in your office.

Example 6.3
Q: When we talk about a concussion of the brain, so as
I understand it, you don't think that that term is
synonymous with mild brain injury?
A: No.
Q: I see on the desk you have a green journal, *The
Journal of Neurology*. Is that a journal that you utilize
in your practice?
A: Yes.
Q: And is it not one of the hotter topics in neurology,
concussion in sports?
A: Did you say hotter or harder?
Q: Hotter?
A: It has been discussed recently, yes.
Q: In fact, I think in the March issue, Drs. Rosenberg
and Kelly wrote an article with regard to concussion in
sports?
A: There were several articles, yes.

Q: Have you read them?

A: Yes.

Q: And am I not correct, that they used the term "concussion" and "mild brain injury" interchangeably?

Lesson: Having the deposition in the expert's office was used against her. The attorney was able to determine that the expert used and read the journal in question. Note that the expert acted properly when she wasn't sure whether the attorney used the word "hotter" or "harder" by asking that the word in question be repeated.

Example 6.4

Q: I see from your diploma that you graduated from MIT in 1991. Your CV says 1989. Which is correct?

Lesson: This question might never had been asked had the deposition not occurred in the expert's office.

Disadvantage 3: The Time of Your Staff

You and your staff will be responsible for cleaning the office and may be called upon to assist at the deposition. This could cost your business time, which translates into money.

Example 6.5

Expert: Let me clean up my desk. Here, you take this chair. Let me get two more chairs. Is a stool okay? You need how many copies of this 29-page document? Here, let me see if I can get a staff member to help us.

Lesson: There may be a cost to your business if you have the deposition in your office.

Disadvantage 4: Availability of On-site Records

You may be called upon to produce additional records or documents that are available on-site. You may or may not be familiar with these documents and you may or may not be prepared to give testimony concerning these records or documents.

Example 6.6

Q: I see the billing information is not in the file you provided. Could you have someone pull the records and bring them in?

Lesson: This request would never be made if the expert was not in her office.

Example 6.7

Q: There's a reference on page one, item number five, of a letter dated October 10, 1995, addressed to Kenneth Webber. Do you have that letter with you?

A: It must be around somewhere.

Q: Can you check your file for me?

A: Yes. Wait a minute.

> **Counsel:** If you are buzzing your secretary, I'd also like the letter of January 12th.
> **Witness:** I'm going to tell her to bring everything in that is out there.
> **Counsel:** Okay.

Lesson: It may be disadvantageous to have a deposition held in your office.

Disadvantage 5: Distractions

You may be distracted by office noise and emergencies. If you are distracted, you are much more likely to slip up.

Disadvantage 6: Less Likely to Prepare

You may be less likely to prepare properly and to focus mentally. If the deposition is in your office, it may subconsciously be considered less of an "event" than if you had to travel for it. You might therefore spend much less time preparing for depositions held in your office.

In the authors' opinion, you may be better served if you have the deposition held in a neutral site out of the office. Counsel may be amenable to this and your travel time may be billable. For the reasons discussed above, it may be to your disadvantage to have the deposition held in your own office. If the deposition is conducted at your office, care should be exercised to use a sterile/bare room so counsel cannot utilize books, articles, diplomas, certificates, and other materials to cross-examine you.

DRESS

If the deposition is being videotaped, you will want to dress appropriately. What is appropriate depends upon how the deposition will be taped and who the jury is likely to consist of. If the deposition is not being videotaped, the jury will most likely never know or care how you dressed for it. In either case, you should put in a quick call to counsel before the deposition and ask her how she would like you to dress.

AVOID ARGUING WITH COUNSEL

There is little, if anything, to be gained by arguing with counsel. Expert witnesses who get emotional and let counsel get under their skin frequently stop thinking clearly about the questions and answers. In video depositions, flashes of anger and quibbling with counsel can adversely affect the credibility of the expert. The more the expert argues with counsel, the greater the risk that she will appear partisan and not impartial.

It is the role of the attorneys in the civil litigation process to argue with each other. Your role is simply to answer the questions. You need to remember these separate and distinct roles and conduct yourself accordingly.

Example 6.8

Q: Sir, would you have a seat, please?

A: If you will have a seat, I will have a seat.

Q: You're in the witness box, sir. You're the witness here.

A: I would ask you to sit down, too.

Q: Sir, there's no requirement that says a lawyer has to sit when listening to a witness. Will you follow the rules of the court, sir, and be seated?

A: Okay. (Expert reluctantly sits down.)

Lesson: The expert has gained nothing by his petty dispute with counsel. He has risked distracting himself and distracting the jury from his opinion.

MAKING DRAWINGS

Counsel may call upon experts to draw diagrams, mark exhibits, or even draw sketches to demonstrate their theories or opinions at deposition. [1]

The sophisticated expert does these drawings or identifications with extreme care and precision to avoid later being impeached by his or her "own hand." When you are asked to draw as opposed to identify, you are well advised to note for the record that this is done freehand, not to scale, and not with precision.

Example 6.9

Q: In that installation you indicated that the support brackets were on the inside of the wheel—of the gear wheel and on the outside, correct?

A: Yes.

Q: And that they went down to a bottom bracket; is that correct?

A: A cross brace, yes.

Q: This is the cross brace here?

A: No, above that.

Q: Would you mark it, please?

A: Yes.

Q: This morning you put an X here.

A: Well—yes.... But I was just approximating it. This is the correct location.

Lesson: The expert's drawing can have as much, or more, impact than his recorded testimony. Drawings and markings should be done carefully with the disclaimer that they are "approximations" and "done freehand."

---

[1] David R. Geiger, et. al, *Deposing Expert Witnesses* (Boston, MA: MCLE, 1993) 7.

Example 6.10
Q: Could you by drawing show us on this bottom bracket where there are bolts?
A: On this bottom bracket?
Q: Yes.
A: Well,—I will do the best that I can freehand, understand.
Q: Do it right here over the conveyor (indicating).
A: Yes.
Q: And you are drawing here the overhead view which you have here?
A: They come through the end. You see the channels here and the holes at the end of the channel....

Lesson: The witness's "freehand disclaimer" was a wise statement to make. She made the disclaimer but was cooperative and did not overplay her hand.

DON'T EXAGGERATE, SPECULATE, GUESS, OR ESTIMATE

You will need to testify with a reasonable degree of certainty. You should not guess, speculate, exaggerate, or estimate. This type of testimony is usually not admissible and can therefore jeopardize your entire opinion. If your testimony is merely a guess, the judge may throw it out of court.

Example 6.11
Q: As I understand it, your opinion is based on your best guess of what happened at the accident scene?
A: That is correct.
> **Deposing Counsel:** Move to strike the testimony of the expert as it is purely speculation and not admissible.

Lesson: This motion may be granted, resulting in the striking of the expert's opinion. "Guessing" is not allowed under the rules of evidence.

INTERRUPTIONS TO QUESTIONS AND ANSWERS

You are well advised not to interrupt questions and blurt out answers even before the question is completed. By doing so you may not be answering the question the lawyer was going to ask you. This may result in an incorrect answer that volunteers information unnecessarily. Additionally, by interrupting the question, you may effectively deny the other lawyers an opportunity to object to the question.

Remember, too, that you are entitled to finish your answer to a question. You should not permit counsel to cut you off when some unexpected or unwanted testimony is about to be delivered.

Example 6.12
Q: You testify for only defendants, isn't that correct?
A: No, that's not correct. As a matter of fact....
Q: Let's move on.
A: I have not finished my answer, counsel. As I was about to say, a full 40% of my work is for plaintiffs.

Lesson: The witness did a good job of not letting the attorney cut off his answer. He made sure he got his answer in the record.

ACTIVELY LISTEN TO THE QUESTION

You need to concentrate intensely on the questions being asked. It is only by listening, hearing, and understanding the question that you can reply honestly and directly. If you do not understand the question, you can and should reply, "I do not understand the question." Use active listening skills. Don't answer the question you anticipate that you are being asked. Answer the question you *are* being asked. It will be counsel's job to clarify or rephrase the question if he or she wishes to do so. Listening and answering the question directly can avoid turning a routine question and answer into a cat and mouse game with a final hesitant and reluctant concession.

Example 6.13
Q: You are an infectious-disease doctor, correct?
A: I'm chairman of infection control at the New England Baptist Hospital, and I've had considerable experience in treating bone and joint infectious diseases during the last 22 years.
Q: Do you consider yourself an infectious-disease doctor?
A: I consider myself to have extensive experience and expertise in the area of bone and joint infectious disease. I do not have boards in infectious disease.
Q: Do you consider yourself, though, an infectious-disease physician?
A: Yes.

Lesson: The jury or fact finder may give this "admission" additional weight due to the manner in which it was elicited. The expert probably would have been better off to answer "Yes" at the start of the questioning.

Don't Memorize Your Testimony
You should be careful about memorizing key answers or testimony. If you do, sophisticated counsel may try to use this testimony against you. Here's how it works.

First, counsel will elicit the same reply at trial that you gave at deposition. She will then ask if the testimony has been memorized. If your reply is in the negative, counsel will then read aloud the verbatim text of the identical reply made at deposition and contained in the deposition transcript. If the jury or fact finder sees the same reply using the same words over and over again, your credibility may be damaged.

OBJECTIONS

When an objection is made, stop talking and listen to the objection carefully. Counsel may, properly or improperly, be signaling you as to the importance of the question and its key elements. Opposing counsel may note his displeasure, but this often is ineffective because the "cat is already out of the bag." If a dispute arises between counsel, you should stay out of it.

Example 6.14
Q: I understand your answer, Doctor, but my question is, if you were to learn that Mr. Jones flexed and extended his wrist, would you concede that his employment would be a risk factor?

> **Retaining Counsel:** Objection. How does he know what—
> **Deposing Counsel:** Please don't coach the witness.
> **Retaining Counsel:** I'm going to object.
> **Deposing Counsel:** Don't make a speaking object, please, Mr. Cone. State your objection and don't educate the witness. I don't appreciate that.

Lesson: The expert in the above case kept his mouth shut and did not get involved in the bickering of the attorneys. After listening to the arguments and objections of the attorneys, he may be better able to answer the posed question accurately.

DON'T GET BURNED "OFF THE RECORD"

Experienced experts may start to feel like lawyers and ask to go "off the record" and say and do things while off the record. Keep in mind that all *off the record* means is that the court reporter is not recording what is said in the deposition transcript. Going off the record means nothing more than this. There is no implied promise, as with a source talking to a reporter, that your off-the-record words will not be used against you. Counsel can and will bring up what was said off the record and not recorded. In addition, in video depositions, an attempt to go off the record can backfire and be portrayed by counsel as an attempt to hide something from the fact finder or the jury. You are well advised not to ask to go off the record. If and when you are off the record, you should not say or do anything that can be used against you.

Example 6.15
Q: Welcome back, sir. Sir, while we were off the record taking a break, you told me that you really can't be sure what happened in this case, didn't you?
A: Ah....
Q: Sir? Did you state that to me?
A: We were off the record!
Q: Did you state that?
A: Let me explain, what I meant was....

Lesson: Going off the record gives you no protection to make confidential comments. Anything you say can and frequently will be used against you.

PAUSE BEFORE ANSWERING

You should pause before answering all but routine questions. *In transcribed depositions there are no points awarded for the speed of your reply because pauses do not show up on the transcribed page.* Pausing serves two important purposes. First, it gives you a chance to consider your response more carefully, and thus reduces the risk of making a misstatement. Second, it gives counsel a better chance of objecting to the question if she so desires. Care should be taken not to overdo this technique, especially in videotape depositions. In videotape depositions, your pause is recorded and may be taken as a sign that you are hesitant or unsure of your replies. In any case, a pause of a second or two between the question and your response is almost always a good idea.

READ AND SIGN

As a deponent, you may, depending upon local rules, have the right to review, correct, and sign the deposition after it has been transcribed. Under the Federal Rules of Civil Procedure, you have the right to review the transcript and make changes in "form or substance."[2] This right is not self-executing, however. In order to assert this right, the expert or the attorney must request reading and signing prior to the completion of the deposition.[3]

You may be asked to waive the right to read and sign. Don't. Experts, especially in high profile litigation, are well advised not to waive the right to review the transcript. In lengthy technical depositions, mistakes are not unusual. You will be given

---

[2] Fed. R. Civ. Pro. 30(e).
[3] Fed. R. Civ. Pro. 30(e).

instructions on how to note your corrections. Follow the instructions precisely.

WHAT TO DO WHEN COUNSEL USES SILENCE

Do not respond to pregnant pauses by counsel. This is a tactic that counsel may use to get or keep you talking. Answer the question before you. After you do, don't say anything until counsel asks another question.

AVOID GESTURING

Do not use gestures, such as nodding or pointing, to respond to a question. Gestures cannot be recorded accurately by the court reporter.

DON'T SHOW WEAKNESS

You should be careful not to give counsel an edge by demonstrating boredom, exasperation, or fatigue. Sophisticated counsel will utilize this information to his or her advantage. By showing weakness, you may prolong the questioning because counsel may keep hammering away at you until you break down and concede all the contested points.

6.2 Maintain the Proper Demeanor

You need to understand that counsel is just as interested in *how* you respond to questions at deposition as in your answers themselves. The lawyers on all sides will evaluate your demeanor in order to determine how effective and credible you will be before a jury or fact finder. The demeanor of the key expert witnesses and their likely effect on the jury are important factors when the lawyers evaluate the case for purposes of possible settlement. Because more than 90% of all contested cases are settled before trial, the demeanor of the expert witness at deposition will have a significant impact on the resultant settlement values. If the case is not settled, your demeanor at deposition will help counsel prepare for your cross-examination at trial. When counsel evaluates your demeanor at deposition, he or she will look first at the 5 C's: *confidence, calmness, control, care,* and *coolness under fire.*

EXUDE CONFIDENCE

You should strive to achieve a professional tone of quiet confidence. Confidence is important because if you do not appear to believe and trust your opinion, how can the lawyers expect the jury to believe your opinion? You should be careful, however, that you don't cross the line from quiet confidence to arrogance. Arrogance can damage your credibility as much as quiet confidence can bolster it.

Example 6.16
Q: Now, Doctor, do you know when was the last time you updated your curriculum vitae?
A: I think it states on the upper right-hand—February 27, 1997.
Q: And your current position at Harramen Hospital?
A: Chief of Obstetrics and Gynecology.
Q: How long have you been you the chief?
A: I've been chief of Obstetrics and Gynecology since the fall of '93 or so, over three years.
Q: Now your CV sets forth various publications that you've been involved in; is that correct?
A: Yes.
Q: How many published works—how many works have you published, do you know? Feel free to look at any exhibit.
A: Between 150 and 200 in total.

Q: And of those 150 and 200 published works, do you know how many refer to fetal distress issues?

A: I would say none.

Q: Have you ever written on any issues concerning fetal distress?

A: I would say no.

Q: And you've never written about fetal hypoxia?

A: That's correct. I've never written about fetal hypoxia.

Q: Have you ever written about fetal acidosis?

A: No.

Q: During the course of a year, how many deliveries are you actively involved in?

A: I personally do about 50 deliveries a year.

Q: And how long have you been doing 50 deliveries a year?

A: Since about 1986.

Lesson: In reading the above exchange, one can almost feel the quiet confidence of the expert. He has no problem in admitting that he has not written about fetal distress or fetal hypoxia. The attorney who cross-examined this expert at deposition did so almost deferentially due to the doctor's acknowledged expertise and quiet air of confidence. This is a valuable expert witness who will probably play well to the jury.

REMAIN CALM, COOL, AND COLLECTED

You will be a much more valuable asset to an attorney if you can stay calm, cool, and collected while under fire at deposition. Such a witness is difficult for counsel to shake, thus removing some of the anxiety and uncertainty about litigation. In order to stay calm, cool, and collected, you need to understand and accept *at the outset of your retention* that difficult questions will be asked and that not everything will go as planned. An ability to handle the unexpected while still maintaining a cool and calm demeanor will help make you an outstanding expert witness. Experts who are flustered easily are less effective and successful at deposition because they may let their emotions take over and misspeak.

Example 6.17
Q: What are the factors one looks at under the DSM-IV for malingering?
A: Gee, I guess we'd have to get it. My memory, I don't have—you know, I know the DSM-IV, I don't have it memorized.
Q: Did you utilize the DSM-IV in coming to an opinion here that Mr. Framo was malingering?
A: Did I utilize it, no. That's a diagnostic manual. I don't think I have to use that as a reference to diagnose malingering. Can I take a break to look at the text?

Lesson: The expert witness was caught off guard, lost his composure, and came off as weak and unsure of himself.

Example 6.18
Q: At the time of the accident, do you know what Mr. Drago's age was?
A: No, I don't.
Q: Do you know what his height was?
A: No, I don't.
Q: His weight?
A: No, I don't.
Q: Past medical history with regard to any preexisting neck or back complaints?
A: No, I don't.

Q: I think you have indicated you don't know his position in the seat?

A: I believe he was the driver but beyond that, no.

Q: You don't know the relationship between Mr. Drago's head with the headrest?

A: No.

Q: Do you know whether the brake was applied?

A: No, I don't and to be perfectly honest, to me that doesn't matter.

Q: Whether a driver is applying a brake in a rear-end collision, would that factor change the length of time of the impact pulse?

A: If they were in fact applying the brake, it would change some circumstances and make the collision milder to the occupants of the vehicle. So, I have taken the worst case.

Lesson: The expert, although under fire, maintains a cool and calm air about him. He is doing well by simply concentrating on answering the questions that are put to him.

MAINTAIN CONTROL

You need to maintain strict control over your responses. To do this, you should concentrate and focus on the questions being asked. Remember, you are an expert, not an advocate. Your role at deposition is quite simple—to truthfully, simply, and directly answer the questions propounded to you. If you maintain control by simply and directly answering the questions you've been asked, you'll be a more credible and more highly valued expert witness.

Example 6.19

Q: Do you know Dr. McConnell?

A: I have met him on a couple of occasions.

Q: Are you familiar with Biodynamic Research Corporation?

A: I'm aware of it.

Q: And they're a company that primarily does work for the insurance and defense industry? By "defense" I mean defense attorneys.

A: Actually, I don't know that. So I can't say that I know that one way or the other.

Q: Are you aware that over a five-year period in the '90's they were paid over seven and a half million dollars by State Farm in the low-impact collisions?

A: No, I wasn't.

Q: Knowing that fact or accepting that fact to be true, would that, in your mind, generate some question as to the validity of the McConnell study?

A: No.

Lesson: Despite being confronted with unexpected questions to which she did not know the answers, the expert maintained her control and did not volunteer any additional thoughts or rationale. She simply focused on the questions and answered them as truthfully and simply as possible. This was a good witness.

AVOID SOUNDING ARROGANT

It is important for the expert witness to guard against any displays of arrogance. There is nothing that will turn off a jury or fact finder quicker than arrogance. Accordingly, you need to be objective about your qualifications but should never be pompous. Remember, the weight to be given to your testimony will ultimately be judged by a jury of lay persons. If they think you are arrogant, it can and will affect your credibility with them. Your testimony is worthless if it is not credible.

To avoid falling into the arrogance trap, try going into the deposition with the mindset of meeting someone for the first time. If you appear arrogant or self-centered, the jury may become turned off quickly. If, on the other hand, you are honest yet humble, you are much more likely to make a good impression. A jury is just like a person you are meeting for the first time. They have little if any prior knowledge of you and they will form a positive or negative impression of you quickly.

Example 6.20

Q: Are you an expert in warnings, sir?

A: Am I an expert? I have written 197 articles and 4 books on warnings. I guess that would make me an expert.

Lesson: "I believe so," or "Yes," are much better responses to this question.

ACT NATURALLY

All expert witnesses are best served by acting naturally and being themselves at deposition. While there is much to be gained by observing skillful and experienced expert witnesses live or on television, experts should be careful to not adopt the latest manner of answering questions. Thus, the best answer to the question, "When did you get your MD degree, doctor?" is not, "To the best of my recollection, on or about June 1997." Likewise, the reply to the question, "Is Ms. Jones your associate?" perhaps should not be answered with, "The answer depends on how you define *is*." Remember, your credibility is an important issue. To maintain your credibility, you should act natural and try not to adopt another person's demeanor or style.

AVOID JOKES AND SARCASTIC OR INAPPROPRIATE
REMARKS

You should not make any jokes, asides, or sarcastic
remarks. These may be misconstrued by a jury or fact
finder and could be used against you by counsel. In
either case, you will probably come off looking
unprofessional. Additionally, the jury may get the
impression that you are not taking the litigation
seriously.

Example 6.21
Q: Tell me about Task Master.
A: That's a computer program that utilizes—primarily
utilizes MODAPTS but it also can use other systems in
assessing work content and work motions and
performing an ergonomic analysis based on the work
content and the worker's motions and movements
required to perform the work task.
Q: Again, is this something that can be used to analyze
any job?
A: Yes, probably, except yours.
Q: Do you personally sell it or is it available through
someone else?
A: It is produced by Grayall Software and I do sell it
and Grayall Software sells it and there are a number of
people that can—
Q: Do you know how much it costs?
A: $950. Would you like to order a copy?

Lesson: It is completely inappropriate for the expert to
attempt to sell counsel software in the midst of his
deposition. Such an inappropriate remark serves no
useful purpose and can only damage an expert's
credibility.

CAREFULLY LISTEN TO AND ANSWER THE QUESTIONS

Being careful is an invaluable asset for any expert deponent. You will need to be very careful in making sure you actively listen to and understand the questions that you are being asked. You also need to be careful to answer the questions accurately, without exaggeration or inaccuracy. If you are careful, you will be less likely to misspeak at deposition. Remember that for depositions that are not videotaped, there are no points given for speed. A delay of a moment or two between the question and your answer will not be reflected in the deposition transcript. Such a delay can help you formulate a carefully considered response.

Example 6.22
Q: Do you know whether or not the Williams text, *Williams on Obstetrics,* sets forth criteria with respect to the pH testing as to whether or not a certain level indicates cesarean delivery?
A: Which text and which edition?
Q: I would say the 18th edition, 1989.
A: No, and I say that because the individuals who wrote the Williams text are not the strongest proponents of doing fetal scalp sampling.

Lesson: The expert made the attorney clarify the question before answering it. The precision and care of the expert in listening to the question and formulating the response are characteristic of an effective and valuable expert witness.

Example 6.23
Q: Well, from your custom and practice in reading these forms, is it fair to say if either represents the time

the culture was taken from the patient or the time it was received by the lab?

A: That would be my best guess.

Lesson: Effective expert witnesses do not guess or speculate. They instead form precise answers based upon their years of expertise. An expert's guess is not likely to play well to the jury. In fact, an expert's willingness to guess may damage his credibility.

Act Dignified and Polite

You need to be polite and maintain your dignity. Experts who maintain their dignity and answer the questions politely are viewed as valuable expert witnesses. Such experts will tend to play well to a jury and are less likely to misspeak. An expert who, on the other hand, continuously jousts with counsel may come off as a partisan who has an ax to grind. Perceived partisanship will damage such an expert's credibility with the jury.

Example 6.24

Q: Please tell me in your own words every reason why you disagree with the OSHA investigator's conclusion as to how the accident in this case happened.

A: I think I have spent quite a few hours explaining it.

Q: Do you know what 40,000-PSI, using that figure, would do to the bones and soft tissues of a hand or arm that passed through such a configuration?

A: Under what condition?

Q: Under the conditions that you have a hydraulically driven conveyor belt with lugs on the under side that passes around a ten inch diameter stainless steel roller and the tissue, the hand and the arm passes all the way around that ten inch roller under the belt?

A: Why don't we cut to the chase here and ask me why his hand wasn't crushed when it went through the roller because that is where you're trying to get and the questions that you're asking don't have a lot to do with engineering. I'll be happy to answer the question I just put to you.

Lesson: The expert has moved away from his role as an impartial expert who should merely answer questions at deposition. This may suggest that he is biased and damage his credibility with the jury. He has also lost his cool and forgotten to simply answer the questions put to him.

DO NOT BE ARGUMENTATIVE

You should not be argumentative. Experts who argue with counsel and who lose their cool and their appearance of impartiality are often ineffective. The jury may get the impression that the reason you are so argumentative is that you have an interest in how the case comes out. Sophisticated counsel are adept at getting under the skin of expert witnesses at deposition. Once the lawyer gets you to be argumentative, you are more likely to volunteer information or to phrase a response inappropriately.

Example 6.25
Q: How would you define HC's relationship to you, what are they to you?
A: They asked me to do this evaluation.
Q: I understand they asked you, what is HC to you?
A: They're an agency that, that wanted me to evaluate her.
Q: One word, can you think of one word that they are to you?

A: You want to give me a multiple choice? I'm not finding a one word that you'd like. Why don't you just tell me what the hell you are looking for and let's get on with it.

      Counsel: I would like to take a break.

Lesson: This is *not* the testimony of a cool, calm, collected, and unflappable expert. A better response might have been, "I'm sorry, but I can't answer that question the way it has been phrased."

DON'T LOSE YOUR TEMPER

Do not allow yourself to be goaded by counsel into losing your temper. If you lose your temper, you will give an emotional response to a question. Such an emotional response will not be carefully considered and will come back to haunt you.

Example 6.26
A: The question you're asking and, again, rather than dance around this for any length of time is what my definition was of mild post-traumatic brain injury. If that's the case, then yes, he had one by definition. But, again, that's a much more encompassing term than is concussion. Yet subjective symptoms of headaches, dizziness, and within several days after the initial injury—so by definition, it's under the general classification of mild post-traumatic brain injury. Whether or not I think he had an initial cerebral concussion, no, I don't.

Lesson: The expert would have been far better served by a cool, calm reply.

Do Not Ramble

Experts who ramble when answering open-ended questions at deposition lack the demeanor of an effective expert witness. An expert who rambles may come off as not being focused and will almost certainly volunteer damaging information. In an attempt to get the witness to ramble, counsel might ask open-ended questions near the end of a deposition when the witness is tired.

Example 6.27

Q: Who is going to have the final say about the care and treatment of Ms. Jones?

A: I'll tell you what my experience is. I see many, many injured workers. I see many individuals with knee problems and I help counsel those individuals as to whether or not they should get certain types of treatment.

Now, I consider myself in a unique position in that I will see a hundred, you know, hundreds of knee injuries come in the door that range from minor to moderate to, you know, more significant to severe and that may include some ligament strains and tears, bursitis, a whole host of things. And I think we'd all agree that probably 90 to 95 percent of them never even get to the orthopedist or the Dr. Fumichs of the world that are standing across the table from me.

Oftentimes I think that because I see such a wide variety of injuries and see the 90 to 95 percent that never get to the surgeon, that oftentimes I'm in a better situation or better position to have a perspective on it to say, hey, this one we've treated conservatively, you know, maybe an injection, some physical therapy, some anti-inflammatories, some bracing, some restricted activities, and they get better whereas some orthopedics, and it's not their fault, obviously, they're going to see a skewed population. They are only seeing the ones that people like me refer to them.

And, for the most part, by the time I have referred them to an orthopedist, you know, the wheels are set in motion that they're going to have surgery because I have already talked with my patient and I feel that they need surgery. That's why I have called the orthopedist in.

So, I don't know, to answer your question, I think it's a difficult question to answer. Who's going to have the final say? I would like to think that at least in my working with orthopedists that I work with, we both have input into it. Obviously I'm not going to do the surgery. So the orthopedist is going to end up scheduling, you know, talking the patient into it or out of it, whatever, for the final decision, and is going to be involved with the scheduling and all that.

I would say probably a more appropriate answer is the patient ultimately decides whether or not they are going to have surgery. We give them recommendations, but ultimately they decide.

Lesson: The expert would have been better served by answering, "The patient ultimately decides himself," rather than rambling.

Example 6.28
Q: Please tell me in your own words every reason why you disagree with the OSHA investigator's conclusion as to how the accident in this case happened.
A: I think I have spent the last twelve hours explaining it.
Q: Would you add anything to what you already said?

A: I have jotted down some notes that I would like to refer to relative to that question and to the extent that I disagree with the OSHA inspector's report that will be responsive to your question.

If you excuse me some of these things we have covered.

I am looking to see if there is any that we have not.

Okay, I also would like the to express the opinion that the wrench has been reported to be on the nut and I find that very unlikely that the wrench can be. The jaws of the wrench can be closed tightly enough on its own or generate enough friction or clamping force to get the needed torque that it would take to bend the wrench as we see here.

Therefore I again don't believe it was on the nut. Also, there has been an opinion expressed most recently by Mr. Lacoque that well perhaps the wrench had slipped between the nut and the frame of the take-up assembly.

I find that from the photographs it is my opinion there is not a sufficient space there for the wrench to fit in that area and if it did it would remove it further from the end of the wrench further from...

Decreasing the likelihood the wrench in fact made contact with the hinge pin.

One opinion that I don't think has been mentioned today or one issue is that the center line of the threaded rod is three inches below the top most edge of the take-up assembly and based on the theory that Mr. Krause was holding the wrench by the head of the wrench at the time it's unlikely that holding it in that position would allow any portion of his thumb to come in contact with the upper most portion of the take-up assembly.

Further, I would express the opinion that based on the reported scenario that the stanchion or the vertical member that we have referred to we know from photographic evidence that it's approximately 12 inches. The closest edge is approximately 12 inches back from the center line of the threaded rod and therefore the stanchion would have likely contacted Mr. Krause's arm above the elbow not some three or four inches above the juncture with his wrist as reported by Mr. Lacoque.

I also found that the stanchion did not act. Or it's my opinion that the stanchion did not act as a guillotine or any type of shearing action for the reason that I have stated and for the fact that it is a single member and there is no cutting action associated with the stanchion.

Additionally, if the thumb had been trapped against the top of the take-up frame the palm of the hand would have been away from the direction of travel of motion of the conveyor and the top portion of the wrench and it was unlikely that the arm would have been pulled at all since the arm in effect was lodged against movement by the pinning action against the take-up frame and let alone there was sufficient force to in fact rip the arm off in that position. I also expressed the opinion that the wrench became dislodged following the energy buildup as reported by Mr. Lacoque and others that the direction of travel of the head of the wrench when Mr. Krause was positioned holding it would have been back towards Mr. Krause due to the actual crimping action of the top portion of the take-up assembly.

I believe we have covered in sufficient detail my opinions relative to the three OSHA regulations that have been cited... 1910.212, 1910.147 and 1910.219 relative to their applicability in this case.

It is further my opinion.... Because we have covered I think in detail what my opinions are relative to the accident scenario.... Hand on the wrench to the roller assembly....

But in addition to that it would be my opinion that the adjustment of the wrench has not been, as shown in the police photos, has not been changed immediately following the accident.

I know we touched on that briefly but I want to express that point again....

Lesson: A better answer might have been, "No, not at this time." That would have probably been the end of the deposition. By letting his frustration get the better of him, the expert rambled, revealed damaging information, boxed himself in at trial, and showed that he can be goaded easily.

6.3 Advice on Answering Questions

AVOID ABSOLUTE WORDS

You are well advised to avoid, where possible, absolute words such as "always" and "never." Absolute words are frequently an invitation to, and fertile grounds for, cross-examination by counsel. Counsel will attempt to damage your credibility by first getting you to make an absolute statement. She will then use counterexamples in an effort to show the falsity of your statement.

Example 6.29
Q: You testified previously that you have read *everything* written on warning labels, isn't that correct?
A: Yes, but that was some time ago.

Lesson: The expert's response here was a good recovery.

Example 6.30
Q: Doctor, it's your testimony that acute stress cannot cause heart attacks under any circumstances, is that correct?
A: It is.
Q: So, Doctor, if I were to reach into my trial bag here (reaches into bag) and pull out a loaded .44 Magnum and point it at your head, and you then had an immediate heart attack, it would be your testimony that the heart attack was not related to stress?

Lesson: The use of absolute words ("any" circumstances) opened the expert up to this sort of cross-examination.

DON'T ELABORATE OR VOLUNTEER

Volunteering information can be one of the biggest mistakes an expert makes at deposition. Generally, an expert should answer only the questions she is asked and not volunteer information. The volunteering of information will almost always result in new lines of cross-examination. It may also disclose information to which counsel otherwise never would have become privy.

Example 6.31
Q: What objective findings of malingering did you make?
A: Lack of atrophy, good muscle tone, oil and grease on his fingernails. There were plenty of subjective findings as well.

Q: Let's get into your so-called subjective findings.

Q: Would you agree with me causation is a medical opinion?

A: Partially.

Q: Okay. (*Note:* No question put to witness, but he answers nonetheless.)

A: If there are idiopathic issues, then it's a medical opinion. If there are not any glaring idiopathic and if a person works in a job that exposes them to risk factors, then I can certainly analyze the job and determine what factors were present and if the person was exposed to those risk factors and barring any other, you know, medical opinion or medical opinion that says, well, there is an idiopathic issue here also, then we assume that the work caused it.

Q: Can you define for me idiopathic carpal tunnel syndrome?

A: Idiopathic causes would be, for example—can be related to diabetes, pregnancy, heart, circulation, even specific anthropomorphics like the size of a person's tunnel, carpal tunnel.

Q: The word idiopathic itself, what does that mean?

A: Well, we'll have to look up the definition.

Q: You'll defer to the dictionary for that.

A: Yes.

Lesson: The witnesses' volunteering of information in both examples opened up new lines of questioning. They should have stopped their answers after their first sentences.

BE CAREFUL WHEN USING HEDGE WORDS

You need to be careful when using *hedge words* when expressing your opinion. Such words include "I guess," "I believe," "it seems," "it's possible," and "I would say." The only reason that you are testifying is to give an opinion. Hedge words and phrases can quickly undermine your opinion and are an invitation for additional cross-examination. Worse, counsel may be able to make a motion to have your entire testimony stricken because expert guessing is not allowed under the rules of evidence.

Example 6.32
Q: That's your "guess," sir?
A: Well, what I meant to say, that it was my opinion that....

Lesson: The expert needed to avoid the hedge words. If he had an opinion he believed in, he should have stated it without employing the hedge words.

CONCESSIONS

In answering questions honestly, you may have to make an occasional concession. If you make the concession graciously and move on, you will exude confidence, integrity, and flexibility. If, on the other hand, you doggedly refuse to give an inch, you may come off as rigid and partisan.

> The most common error the beginning expert makes in a deposition is the failure to concede an obvious and irrefutable point out of misguided loyalty to his or her side of the case.... Quibbling over the possible exceptions or equivocating in some way helps no one.[4]

---

[4] Thomas G. Gutheil, *The Psychiatrist as Expert Witness* (Washington, DC: American Psychiatric Press, 1998) 69, 71–72.

Example 6.33

Q: Now, would you agree just because the Glasgow Coma Scale was 15, there were no focal neurological deficits, that one still cannot rule out whether or not Mr. Framo had suffered a concussion or mild brain injury?
A: That's correct. He could have.

Lesson: When an expert makes a concession promptly without the necessity of a long series of leading questions, the concession's effect on the jury or fact finder is reduced.

Example 6.34

Q: If somebody does a flexion and extension movement making half a million pieces a year, Doctor, would that be significant enough to cause someone to get carpal tunnel syndrome from their job?
A: Again, I would have to look at the specific flexion-extension activity, but certainly that degree of flexion-extension activity at the wrist, one would have to consider that as a, you know, a cause or a contributing factor.
Counsel: Thank you. That's all I have.

Lesson: When the expert fights the concession every inch of the way and concedes only when left no reasonable alternative explanation, the concession is emphasized. Counsel frequently use such a concession to conclude the deposition with a flourish.

"I DON'T KNOW"

If you are asked a question that you do not know the answer to, your answer should be, "I don't know." There is absolutely nothing wrong with this response if you genuinely do not know the answer to the question.

There are probably thousands of questions that can be asked of experts in any discipline to which they have no answer. The more the expert hesitates or tries to avoid saying, "I don't know," the more emphasis is given to this "lack of knowledge" by the jury or fact finder. No amount of hesitation will bring the answer to you if you do not know it.

Example 6.35
Q: What is the coefficient for friction for steel on cement?
A: I don't know.

Lesson: The forthright admission of lack of knowledge was in the expert's best interest. Had the expert tried to talk around this, it would have only emphasized her lack of knowledge.

Example 6.36
Q: If those wrist rests were unavailable prior to 1991, would you agree she had a higher probability then of being in a neutral position?
A: I don't know. That's an interesting question. I don't know. I mean I guess that's my answer, I don't know. But I think the wrist rests certainly emphasizes, even though you have the Ridyard's ergonomic assessment of 1994, if Miss Sanford and/or her supervisor were trained, that would not have been a product of choice.

Lesson: If you allow yourself to get flustered, your lack of knowledge will be emphasized to the jury. The expert in this example would have been better served by replying, "I don't know" and then sitting quietly and waiting for the next question.

"I DON'T RECALL"

When asked about a fact, situation, or occurrence that you honestly do not remember, the best answer is, "I do not remember" or "I don't recall." This is only an appropriate answer when you honestly have no recollection. Perjury ramifications aside, an endless string of "I don't recalls" (or even one that may seem hard to believe) may tend to damage your credibility.[5] If your response is that you do not recall, counsel may then attempt to refresh your memory. This is permissible under the rules of evidence.

Example 6.37

Q: Doctor, do you have any memory, independent of the medical records, of any of the events that occurred on August 5 of 1990, regarding the treatment of Ms. Lynn?

A: I would say no. Can't really remember any real specifics on that particular day. I remember snatches of her. Over her two-year course, I recall her and various things over a two-year span, but that particular day I can't recall any real specifics.

Q: Have you reviewed the medical record of August 5, 1990, from the emergency room, the Baystate Medical Center?

A: Yes, I have.

Q: Does that medical record refresh your memory in any way as to where you were approximately the time

---

[5] For example, **Q:** Were you ever alone with Monica Lewinsky? **A:** I don't recall.

that she was admitted to the hospital about 4 A.M. on that day?

A: She came in at 4 A.M. that morning. The reading doesn't refresh my memory.

Q: Does the record indicate approximately when you first appeared on August 5 at Baystate Medical Center?

A: Just looking at it very quickly now, looked at this in detail earlier, I don't see anything in the record in and of itself that refreshes my memory on when I physically was present, near Ms. Lynn or in her care. I don't see anything that would indicate an exact time.

Lesson: As noted above, if the document does not refresh your memory or recollection, you are free to so testify. In this case, counsel was forced to drop this line of inquiry and move on.

BEWARE OF OPEN-ENDED QUESTIONS

You should be cautious when dealing with open-ended questions. These questions invite long, rambling answers. Counsel may be trying to get you to volunteer information not called for by the question. If you do volunteer information, it is likely that this information will be used against you during cross-examination. You should therefore answer open-ended questions as concisely as possible, being careful not to provide information that was not asked for.

Example 6.38

Q: What do you consider to be the unsafe uses of an ATV?

A: Oh.... I can give you some highlights. There are many, many unsafe uses, but classic unsafe use is as a mobile transport form to transport you and a loaded firearm. This is not a motorized attack vehicle. It is not a multi-passenger transport vehicle, although it has to be conceded that because of its stability and because of its wide platform, you can safely transport a passenger on it. You just have to be more careful. But that is not a correct use of the vehicle, so depending—it's like everything else. You could probably even transport a loaded firearm safely if you took enough precautions, so when I say unsafe use, it's not a recommended use, not that you can't pull off that maneuver safely with enough care.

Certainly you could easily find loads and pulling tasks like stumps that just by their nature the vehicle was not designed to do, and people will try and use the dynamics of the vehicle to run up against the rope and jerk on something really hard and say—but that's not a good idea.

It is not for transport on paved roadways. I mean, you can drive it. It will run. The traffic cops in Hawaii write all their parking tickets on three-wheeled ATVs with tires scrubbed smooth, and you can do that safely, but that's just not a recommended use. I mean, you are—you are....

I think it's fair to say unless you know what you're doing, it is not a competitive speed machine. I mean, there are...people race it and, and...most people don't have any business racing cars. It doesn't mean they don't do it, but that is potentially a hazardous use.

They are not vehicles...for—I don't know how to characterize this...I'm going to say not very well thought out horseplay. That's an inelegant statement, but you see uses of these vehicles for games like chicken and...sort of it's horses substitutes for games. I mean, they are not a horse. I mean I don't mean that pejoratively. Horses, because they have their own will, they have their own unique set of problems, but an

ATV is not a horse, and attempting to use it like one can be a misuse of it.

And finally, I guess, an ATV is not a toy. Anything with a multiple horsepower engine is not a toy in the sense that classic things people think of as a toy is something you can drop—drop in the crib or playpen, and, you know, it ain't one of those. It's a vehicle that has the capability of putting energy at the command of anybody…tall enough to reach the handle bars and the accelerator and the gear shift or long enough legs to reach the gear shift, and the people who ergonomically fit that envelope do not overlap totally with the people whose judgment is appropriate for operating one of these, and so use of it as a toy, as a toy substitute, is not appropriate.

Now, obviously, every one of those categories has bits of infinite detail, numerous scenarios.

Lesson: Note the numerous areas of inquiry opened up by this long, rambling answer to a single open-ended question. Experts are better served by brief, succinct replies to open-ended questions. If counsel has follow-up questions, let her ask them. Don't do the lawyer's job for her.

AVOID SLANG

Avoid slang expressions when replying to questions. When they are transcribed and read back to a jury, these expressions diminish the value of your reply and can make you sound almost illiterate. Most slang expressions slip from experts unintentionally. To avoid making such a slip, you will need to maintain your concentration and focus.

Example 6.39

Q: Now, sir, you were asked on direct examination about the history that you took from Ronald Evans, right?

A: Uh-huh.

Q: And the history is the story that he tells you, correct?

A: Uh-huh.

Q: Is that a yes?

A: Yes, it is.

Q: And you told us that Mr. Evans told you that he hurt himself while lifting some boxes at work?

Q: Uh-huh, I mean, yes.

Q: Are you familiar with an organization called M.O.R. Incorporated, sir?

A: Nope.

Lesson: The expert's use of slang cheapens his testimony and diminishes his credibility.

COUNSEL'S "BUMBLE AND FUMBLE" GAMBIT

Do not help counsel when he is apparently bumbling or fumbling with some type of technical question. Experts are frequently tricked into volunteering key information by such real or feigned ignorance. Let counsel bumble or fumble all they want. Remember, you are there to answer questions, not to assist counsel in framing them correctly.

YES OR NO RESPONSES

If counsel asks for a yes or no response and you can answer the question with a yes or a no, endeavor to do so. If counsel attempts to insist on a yes or no answer to questions that cannot be answered in that fashion, you can state, "I cannot answer that question with a yes or no reply." It will then be up to counsel to either let you explain your answer or rephrase his question.

WHAT TO DO WHEN YOU MAKE A MISTAKE

Expert witnesses are not expected to be perfect. During a long and arduous deposition, you may misspeak or make a mistake or error. If you do make a mistake, you should correct the error on the record as soon as you recognize your error. "I want to correct a statement I made a few minutes ago. I stated that the 1991 EMG was related to the surgery. That is incorrect." Counsel may quickly challenge you on your mistake before you have an opportunity to correct it. In that case, admit your error graciously. What you want to avoid after making a mistake is making the matter even worse by your inability or unwillingness to admit the mistake. This could make you look biased. If you discover your mistake after the deposition concludes, notify counsel and correct the deposition transcript when it comes for your signature.

Example 6.40
Q: You only treated her for a 1981 accident, correct?
A: You know, it's interesting, I'm looking at what we wrote down here and it says "1981-1984 motor vehicle accident, recovered." I may have misinterpreted what this note was. The accident was in '81, but we saw her in '84; and I apologize if I misled you.

Lesson: The expert has done a good job handling his mistake. He comes off as human, and above all, honest.

Example 6.41

Q: Your comment was that the normal EMG in 1991 related to the surgery. Now, that doesn't make sense, does it?

A: Did she have surgery in the interim?

Q: No, she did not.

A: You're correct, it doesn't make sense. Well, it doesn't necessarily not make sense, either, because after surgery for a carpal tunnel syndrome, the EMG changes can wax and wane. You can have EMG positive one month and a year later negative. It may be a direct result of the surgery. My statement may still hold up, but I made that statement in error.

Lesson: The expert here may come off as inflexible, closed-minded, or biased. Either way, he lessens his credibility by trying to explain away his misstatement.

"I DON'T KNOW, BUT..."

As an expert witness, you are under oath to tell the truth. You should not speculate, but should testify with a reasonable degree of certainty. At deposition, many experts do not practice this principle and, in fact, speculate freely. One of the most common forms of speculation by experts at deposition is the "I do not know, but..." reply. It is usually a mistake to use this response. First of all, if you don't know, then any information you provide after the "but" is mere speculation. Secondly, you may volunteer damaging information after the "but."

Example 6.42

Q: Do you know whether or not GM employed any other method to determine longitudinal velocity of test dummies?

A: I don't know if we compute longitudinal velocity based on accelerometers, but I suppose you could.

Lesson: The simple, direct, and best response is, "I don't know." The throwaway statements that come after the "but" or "I don't know" reply help counsel by providing him or her with additional information. This type of reply frequently results in new lines of inquiry and detailed questioning by counsel.

Example 6.43
Q: Do you know, in this crash test, what causes the voltage drop and rise?
A: I don't know but that's typically an indication that the switch is opening and closing.
Q: When you say opening and closing, sir, would you explain what you mean in this context?

Lesson: By providing a "but," the witness has opened a new line of questioning. This was probably avoidable simply by answering the question, "I don't know" or "No."

Example 6.44
Q: Why does crash test 4665 have such charts and the remaining frontal barrier tests do not?
A: Well, I don't really know, but if you would like me to review the other tests to determine whether or not those tests have such—I can certainly do that, but I guess this one had switches, and they must have been requested.

Lesson: This witness has answered, "I don't know" and then made an offer to assist counsel. The simple, most accurate, and best reply is, "I don't know." Any comments made as an afterthought are unwise, unprofessional, and inconsistent with being successful as an expert at deposition.

"HOPING"

Sophisticated counsel may attempt to trap the expert witness by the use of the word *hope*. If you inadvertently agree with a characterization, you may allow the lawyer to successfully call into question the reliability of your opinion. When you are confronted with an "And you are hoping..." question, it may be best to actively refute that characterization. Remember that when you are passive and agree to an attorney's characterization or mischaracterization, you are in effect letting the attorney put words in your mouth.

Example 6.45

Q: Doctor, one more thing. Your opinion here today that Mr. Stanek has asked you about, in part, is based on the history that you get from the patient, isn't that correct, and your training, obviously?

A: Yes, sure.

Q: And you're hoping, of course, as most doctors, that the patients are accurate when they give you a history and tell you what's wrong with them. Is that a fair statement?

A: Yes.

Lesson: Counsel has raised questions in the minds of the jury or fact finder regarding the reliability of the history (i.e., assumptions upon which the expert's opinion was based). "Hoping" may be made to seem akin to "guessing." A better answer might have been,

"I don't 'hope' that I was provided an accurate history,
I assume so unless I have reason to suspect otherwise."

REFUSAL TO SPECULATE

You should not permit yourself to be tricked, cajoled,
or forced into speculating when answering questions
under oath at deposition. There is nothing wrong with
the response, "I'm sorry, but I'm not going to speculate
on that."

Example 6.46
Q: So what you're saying here is that this coated cable
itself is what deflected?
A: That is correct.
Q: And is it also correct to say that when you ran that
test that a portion of that coated cable was left outside
of the interlocking portion of the lacings?
A: It would be correct to say that that assembly as
purchased was assembled based on our understanding
and also whatever instructions that came with it so there
was an equal portion sticking out of either end. The
exact length of the cable beyond the lacing what we
refer to as the hinge device I can't give you a dimension
on that. I don't really recall.
Q: Was there some portion of it?
A: My recollection that the washer was crimped on the
metal cap and to what extent the cable stuck out I
couldn't theorize at this point.
Q: Can you say whether it did or whether it didn't to
any extent?
A: I can't with any accuracy.
Q: I am not asking for any millimeters.
A: I understand. I can't speculate that it did or did not
at this point.

Lesson: The expert did an excellent job of not allowing himself to be pushed into speculating.

"POSSIBILITY"

Beware of the use of the word *possible*. Testifying that something is merely "possible" is most likely legally insufficient.[6] If your opinion is only a mere possibility, the judge will most likely not allow it to be presented to the jury as evidence.

Example 6.47

Q: Is it your testimony that Ms. Cain's carpal tunnel syndrome is causally related to her employment as a stitcher at Johnson Company, Doctor?

A: It's possible.

Q: If I were to say to you, today, that at 4:00 this afternoon, on January the 12th, 1994, here in Buffaloe, New York, it's going to be sunny, 90 outside and we're all going to go swimming, that's a possibility, isn't it?

A: That's a possibility.

Q: That's not a probability?

A: That's not a probability.

Q: So, a probability is something more likely than not; is that correct?

A: That's correct.

Q: So, when you say something is probable, you're saying that something is more likely than not, am I correct in understanding this?

A: If it's probable, it's more likely than not.

Q: And possible means—well, anything is possible?

---

[6] Generally speaking, your opinion must be based upon a reasonable degree of certainty for it to be legally sufficient to submit to a jury. If it is not based upon a reasonable degree of certainty, the judge can and will exclude it from evidence.

Counsel: Object, as leading.
Q: Well, how would you define possible, Doctor?
A: Possible, I would say something is possible, if there's some likelihood it may happen, even though it's remote. Or one of many likelihoods that, something will happen.
Q: So, we're talking about, essentially something that one can, the difference is, probable is whether you can stake a bet on it. Possible, you might not stake a bet on it?
A: Yeah. In layman's language, that's good.

Lesson: When an expert witness at deposition uses the terms *possible* or *possibly,* he or she can reasonably expect the above line of questioning by counsel. If the lawyer can show that your opinion is only based on a mere possibility, he may succeed in excluding your opinion from being admitted into evidence at trial.

"I GUESS"

As an expert, you are testifying under oath. Your testimony will help resolve the rights and liabilities of parties who are involved in a legal dispute. Accordingly, there is no place for you to guess. Experts are well advised to leave the guessing to financial advisers, political pundits, and meteorologists.

Example 6.48
Q: What would the purpose be of increasing spool diameter, sir?
A: Well, I'm not sure why they did it in that case. I guess there could be as many reasons as there are diameters of spools.
Q: Mr. Green, what caused the damage to the throttle valve on the accident ATV?

A: I don't really know for sure, but my best guess was that it was misassembled by the distributor.

Q: Essentially the seat is part of the restraint system, is that correct, sir?
A: Well, I guess the restraint system consists of the belts and their attachment points within the vehicle. That leaves out the seat.

Q: In this case you did work for a company called Comp Management, Inc., correct?
A: Yes.
Q: And you've done other work for them?
A: I guess so.
Q: Well, yes or no?
A: I don't know.

Lesson: Your "guesses" are not admissible in evidence. Guessing can only hurt your credibility. It should be avoided.

"I DON'T UNDERSTAND THE QUESTION"

You need not answer questions that you do not understand. If the question propounded to you is confusing, the preferred answer is, "I don't understand the question." Exercise caution in giving "I don't understand" replies to avoid answering questions improperly. For example, if you are one of the leading computer experts in the world and have testified that you didn't understand a question about a browser, it is likely that your credibility will be impaired. You must answer truthfully and are permitted to answer, "I don't understand" only when that is the actual case.

Example 6.49

Q: Do you know whether or not GM vehicles manufactured prior to 1995 ever incorporated a retractor assembly with a limitation on the amount of slack that could be produced into the shoulder harness webbing?

A: I don't understand.

Q: Let me try and rephrase the question.

Lesson: When the expert legitimately answers, "I don't know," counsel is forced to rephrase the question or move on. By only answering questions that you understand, you will help ensure that the testimony you give is accurate and not misleading.

COMPOUND QUESTIONS

Frequently, attorneys attempt to confuse the expert at deposition by asking *compound questions;* that is, two questions combined. Sometimes the question is asked in a stream of consciousness manner that is difficult to comprehend, let alone answer accurately. When faced with such questions, appropriate responses include: "Counsel, you have asked several questions. Can you simplify the question so I can answer it accurately?" and, "Counsel, I'm sorry, I don't understand the question. Could you please rephrase it?"

Example 6.50

Q: Well, I guess what I'm having trouble with is you have concluded that he's malingering, there's nothing wrong with him. Yet on a test, for instance, that tests the ability of a person to be conceptual, he gives an answer which in and of itself you didn't think showed malingering. I'm trying to understand how he has all these difficulties and how you come to the conclusion that the answers that he gave that were incorrect show malingering.

A: Counsel, you have asked several questions. Can you simplify the question so I can answer it accurately?

Lesson: The expert provided a good response to counsel's question.

Example 6.51

Q: In those cases where there was one for the plaintiff or the treating doctor and the second for a defense neuropsychologist, the fact that the test results—you determined the test results were invalid because there's no—not that consistency, does that invalidate the first testing? Can you determine—if you see two inconsistent tests, does that mean both are invalid or the first may be valid and the second invalid?

A: That's a complicated question to which I don't have a definitive answer. I can say that on many of the tests the average scores for the first testing and the second testing were not significantly different; in other words, they did about equally as well. Although, I have to make clear that the scores on the second testing, while not significantly different statistically, did tend to be a little lower than the scores on the first testing. And looks like—it would look like that under pressure of litigation with the second testing coming up, perhaps when trial was coming close or something of that sort, that these people were just not able to put forth quite as good a performance as they did on the first testing. But at the same time the scores were generally—they were not strikingly different. The inconsistency, the intraindividual inconsistency were the striking elements of differences between the two testings.

Lesson: A better answer might have been, "I don't know." As you might expect, the answer given opened up several new areas of inquiry.

"I ASSUME"

You should not make unfounded or unsupported assumptions in an attempt to answer a question. If you can't answer or don't know the answer, say so. Expert witnesses need not and should not make unsupported or unsubstantiated assumptions in an attempt to answer questions at deposition.

Example 6.52
Q: Does the computer program have the capability of printing out a master index of all of the crash tests?
A: I don't know, but I would assume that some computer person set this system up and can go in and generate a list of all of the data in there....

Lesson: Assuming in a case like this is akin to guessing and should be avoided. A better answer might have been, "I don't know."

6.4 Breaks

Giving testimony at a deposition is much easier than testifying at trial. One reason for this is that it is much more likely that you will be granted a break if you request one. Ask for a break or recess any time you want one, need one, or feel that it will help you collect your thoughts so that you can return reinvigorated. Don't let yourself get distracted by an urge to use the restroom or call your spouse to check in on a sick relative. If you need a break, ask for it. Remember, however, that who you talked to and what you talked about during a break may be the subject of close questioning when the deposition resumes.

Example 6.53
Q: Doctor, I take it you just had lunch with counsel?
A: I did.
Q: What about this case did you just discuss?
A: I don't know if we discussed it at all. What about the case? I don't think we mentioned Miss Sanford's name. I talked about the railroads in general.
Q: Did you talk about the reservation sales office at all?

Lesson: You should expect to be questioned about what was discussed with counsel at lunch and during other breaks in the deposition.

The sophisticated expert witness understands how and when to utilize a request for a break to his or her advantage. A request for a break can help the expert in several ways. He or she can:

- regain his or her composure,
- rest and recover the ability to concentrate,
- stretch, and
- recover the will to continue an arduous deposition.

Some experts make an issue of taking a "macho" approach to breaks. They think, "I am one tough SOB and do not need any breaks."

Example 6.54
Q: Doctor, you were sort of parched before. Do you need to take a break to have a drink or something?
A: I don't need a break, but go ahead and I'll drink while you ask questions.

Lesson: This "macho" approach is counterproductive because it signals not toughness, but the propensity to be manipulated easily by counsel. Note how the above question was phrased, "Do you *need* a break?" Here the expert has placed himself at a physical disadvantage by not taking a short break.

STRATEGY

Frequently, expert witnesses make the mistake of going on without a break just to get the deposition over with. Psychologically, this is a crucial error. Experts start to concentrate not on the questions and their answers, but on how much longer the deposition will go on. This situation can become even more severe if the expert has not left himself adequate time and is rushing to get to another appointment. Once counsel senses that the expert is pressed for time, she will capitalize on that fact and use it as a tactical advantage.

Example 6.55
Q: I notice you are looking at your watch. Are you OK on time?
A: Well, I do have a 5:00 P.M. flight out of O'Hare and with the traffic from downtown.... It is 3:45....
Q: I only have a few more questions.... We should be done in fifteen minutes.

Lesson: What counsel is really saying is, "If you cooperate, you will make your plane. If not, who knows?" The expert is well advised to leave herself adequate time for the deposition.

      The judicious use of a break by an expert witness can sometimes be the psychological turning point in a lengthy and contentious deposition. In *The Hustler*, the young pool player (Paul Newman) beats the veteran (Jackie Gleason) for hours on end. Gleason, playing Minnesota Fats, takes a break, changes his shirt, combs his hair, and comes out refreshed and seemingly ready to start all over. Newman looks in the mirror, sees he is disheveled and exhausted, and begins to lose. He continues to lose until he runs out of money. This was the psychological turning point in the match.

      Taking periodic breaks to refresh and gird oneself for the continuing mental strain of a deposition sends an important signal to counsel. It shows that you will not allow yourself to be ground down and made to capitulate due to exhaustion, time constraints, or just because you want to get the deposition over with.

CONSULTING WITH COUNSEL

It is very tempting for an expert to take a break with the hope of being able to consult with counsel concerning a crucial line of inquiry. This is a serious mistake. Anything you discuss with counsel during a break can and frequently will become a matter of inquiry during the deposition.

Example 6.56
Q: During the ten-minute break, did you talk to Attorney Jones?
A: Yes.

Q: Did you discuss this case?

A: Well...just generally.

Q: What did you say and what did Attorney Jones say?

Lesson: This is a legitimate line of inquiry. If you discuss the case during a break, you can and will be questioned about these conversations.

Example 6.57

Q: Now that you have had fifteen minutes to consult with counsel, do you have an answer to the question of whether your professional license was ever suspended?

Lesson: Sometimes counsel will take a cheap shot and ask this type of question after a break. If you did not discuss the case, counsel should object and note his or her displeasure with this tactic.

PLAYING WITH EQUIPMENT EXHIBITS

Experts should remember that anything that they say or do during a break may be, and in many cases will be, used by counsel to bolster his or her case. This may include making notes, doodling on a legal pad, or playing with equipment or exhibits.

Example 6.58

Q: Mr. Floyd, when we just had a break you were standing over by the old file cabinets here...you picked up the wrench. What did you do with the wrench when you picked it up?

A: I opened the jaws and I closed them back and I believe I laid it back down.

Q: Why did you do that?

A: Because engineers are curious people.

Q: Is it fair to say that anybody with some mechanical aptitude is curious when they pick up a wrench there is a tendency to adjust the jaws?

A: I can't see that in any likelihood that when Mr. DiMaggio pried this wrench out of Mr. Clark's hand that he checked to see if the jaw mechanism of this wrench still worked.

Q: What about somebody other than Mr. DiMaggio?

A: The only other person reported to be around that machine was Officer Juscowitz who is trained obviously in the gathering of evidence and so forth so I find it unlikely that he changed the jaw setting.

Q: But that is the first thing you did when you picked up the wrench, correct?

A: That is correct.

Lesson: Experts are well advised not to tinker with the exhibits during breaks in the deposition.

Chapter 7 Setting Your Fee, Billing, and Collecting

7.1 Your Fee

WHO IS RESPONSIBLE TO PAY YOUR FEE

Under the Federal Rules of Civil Procedure, the party seeking to depose you as an expert witness is liable for your fee.[1] The reasonable fee you can charge counsel may includes travel costs. What is a *reasonable* fee for being deposed? In the case of *Anthony v. Abbot Laboratories* 106 F.R.D. 461 (1985), the court utilized 10 factors to determine what was a reasonable fee.

1. the location of the deposition was chosen to suit the convenience of the witness;
2. a timely objection was made to the amount of the fee;
3. the credentials possessed by the witness;
4. whether the deposition was being obtained on very brief notice or with adequate lead time;
5. the going rates in the area where the deposition was being taken;
6. whether the witness was one of few persons with qualifications and expertise to testify on the matters in issue (in this case, the causative effects of diethylstilbestrol);

---

[1] Fed. R. Civ. Pro. 26(b)(4)(c) states:
Unless manifest injustice would result, (i) the court shall require that the party seeking discovery pay the expert a reasonable fee for time spent in responding to discovery under this subdivision; and (ii) with respect to discovery obtained under subdivision (b)(4)(B) of this rule the court shall require the party seeking discovery to pay the other party a fair portion of the fees and expenses reasonably incurred by the latter party in obtaining facts and opinions from the expert.

7. what the witness charges or has charged a "friendly litigant" as opposed to the adversary;
8. whether there was any showing of manifest inconvenience;
9. whether there was any showing of consequential loss; and
10. whether the witness has any discernible overhead.[2]

The expert who attempts to charge a fee that is unreasonable is subject to counsel moving for a protective order and obtaining a strict limit on his hourly fee. This is especially true if an expert tries to charge a higher fee for the deposition than he is charging the party that retained him for other time in the case.[3] Often, counsel will consult with the expert on the fee and work out an agreement with little or no difficulty. In some cases this is noted on the record.

Example 7.1
Q: Do you have an agreement generally for compensation for your services in this case?
A: Mr. Hanyen is aware of what I charge for my services if that constitutes an agreement.
Q: With whom do you have an agreement?
A: With Mr. Hanyen.
Q: What are your normal charges?
A: $250 an hour.
Q: Are they any different for the deposition?
A: No, sir.

---

[2] James L. Branton and Jim D. Lovett, *Depositions* (Ft. Worth, TX: Knowles Publishing, Inc., 1998) W10.
[3] There is generally no legal limit to this fee.

Lesson: The expert is charging the same hourly rate for the deposition as she charges counsel for the party who has retained her. There is no dispute or problem.

If you decide to raise your hourly fee because opposing counsel is taking the deposition, this may create problems. An attempt to gouge opposing counsel is ethically and legally suspect and may result in intense cross-examination. It could also damage your credibility at deposition.

Example 7.2
Q: All right. What is the scale that you charge for depositions that are taken here at your offices in Pennsylvania, Doctor, and you can look at the exhibit that gives a breakdown of your deposition fees, sir.
A: Oral deposition, first hour $600.
Q: Okay. And what is the cost for attorney time?
A: Attorney conference, first half-hour $150.
Q: And what is the cost of a video deposition, sir?
A: The first hour $800.
Q: And what is the cost for each additional hour after the first hour?
A: Will be charged at the same rate as the first hour but will be charged in 15-minute increments.
Q: Okay. And Doctor, you require a deposit of $500 in advance of taking your deposition, correct?
A: That's correct.
Q: And if that $500 is not paid in advance of the time that your deposition is scheduled, the deposition will be cancelled, correct?
A: That's correct.
Q: All right. You said that you do not recall the fee that you required that I pay to take your discovery

deposition a few weeks ago, Doctor, and I want to hand you this and ask if you recognize this as being part of the stationery from your office, sir?

A: Yes.

Q: All right. Is that a bill?

A: It's one of the sheets of a bill, yes.

Q: Okay. And that bill is made out to who?

A: Wallace & LoPresti, Attorneys at Law.

Q: Okay. And you recognize that as being my firm, correct?

A: Yes.

Q: Okay. And the charge at the bottom here says what?

A: $750.

Q: So in fact you raise your fees when opposing counsel takes your deposition?

A: That's ridiculous.

Q: You attempted to overcharge for this deposition also, did you not?

A: I charged a reasonable fee.

Q: Didn't you receive any of the correspondence from the court regarding the issue that we had about your fees for deposition?

Objection.

Q: Cost of services, sir?

Objection.

A: I had looked at it before referring it to my attorney, yes.

Q: Okay. You referred the matter to your attorney, right, Doctor?

Objection.

A: That's correct.

Q: And the court reduced your fee pursuant to my request, correct?

A: That's correct.

Lesson: This is not the recommended way to start a discovery deposition. Had the expert charged a reasonable fee instead of attempting to charge opposing counsel an increased amount, the above interchange could have been avoided. Experts should check to see if local court rules or practices dictate the parameters for what a reasonable fee is.

WHAT YOU CAN CHARGE FOR

An in-depth discussion of expert witness and consulting fees is beyond the scope of this work. However, the authors have one piece of general advice relating to getting paid fairly for your work. That advice is: **Bill as an attorney would bill had you retained the attorney instead of vice versa.** You need to keep in mind that attorneys are generally the ones that retain you as an expert witness. When you have been hired by an attorney, you should not hesitate in billing the attorney exactly as she would bill you had you retained *her* professional services. If you have not worked for the attorney or firm before, however, it may be a good idea to explain how you will be billing and what you will be billing for at the outset of your engagement. You can and in most cases should bill for the following.

1. *All time spent on the case.* This includes, but is not limited to, research, telephone calls (even if brief), preparation time, reading and signing the deposition, testifying time, time drafting reports, time spent responding to subpoenas, and travel time. Remember, an attorney would charge you for every bit of time she spent on your case. You shouldn't hesitate to do the same.
2. *Out-of-pocket expenses.* These include travel expenses, photocopying, electronic

research, and telecommunications. This is
how attorneys would bill you. They are
therefore in a weak position to complain if
this is how you bill them.

If you are billing the opposing side for
deposition-related expenses, the law may impose limits
regarding what you can bill for.[4] There is generally no
harm in attempting to bill the side who deposes you for
travel and reading and signing time. You never know
what you might get until you ask!

HOW MUCH YOU CAN CHARGE

The only limit to how much you can charge for your
time is *reasonableness.* Reasonableness comes into
play in three ways. First, it may be a legal limitation, as
discussed above. Second, the marketplace will
generally not allow experts to charge an unreasonable
rate. Third, a rate that is above a certain level may
cause a backlash and lost credibility with the fact
finder.

The authors recommend that you be prepared to
justify the reasonableness of your fee. ***With proper
justification, a very high fee can quickly be made to
look fairly reasonable.*** The 10 points from the *Anthony
v. Abbot Laboratories* case given at the beginning of
this chapter are a good place to start. Your fee should
be found to be reasonable if you can justify the value of
your time objectively. For example, if traveling to a 3-
hour deposition will cost you $5,000 in lost surgery

---

[4] See, e.g., *M.T. McBrian, Inc. v. Liebert Corp.,* 173 F.R.D. 491
(N.D. Ill. 1997). (Travel, lodging expenses, and preparation time
are not recoverable where the travel of an expert was at the
retaining party's request and the case was not complex with a
considerable lapse of time between the expert's work on the case
and the date of the deposition.)

billables, plus overhead, you should be able to charge a substantial fee for your time at the deposition. If, however, you are a retired physician who hasn't operated in fifteen years, you may have more difficulty in justifying an unusually large fee.

7.2 Billings and Collections

Most experienced expert witnesses strongly recommend that experts be paid prior to giving a deposition. *This is the only way to guarantee collection of your fees.* The expert who does not demand payment in advance will run the risk of late payment, no payment, and/or collection problems with counsel. If you are charging an hourly rate, estimate the time and obtain an amount sufficient to avoid having to chase the lawyer after the deposition is completed. Many experts make a certain percentage of the fee nonrefundable if the deposition is cancelled or postponed on short notice. This technique can be very useful in protecting the expert from losing the value of the time blocked off for the deposition. If the deposition goes longer than anticipated, the expert can put his fee concerns on the record tactfully.

Example 7.3
A: Counsel, you estimated two hours and that is how much I was paid for. Do you agree to pay for the additional time involved within ten days?
Q: Yes, that's fine. Let's proceed.

Lesson: Getting an agreement to pay your fees on the record may be helpful if collection difficulties arise after the deposition.

If you are not paid in advance for the deposition, you should *promptly* submit your bill for payment. This is helpful in securing collection for two reasons. First, if you are not paid, you can attempt collection while the litigation is ongoing. You will have the most leverage to collect while the matter is still pending before the court. Second, the attorney is more likely to pay you if you bill her promptly. When a bill is sent late, especially after a case has been lost, collection problems may arise.

Chapter 8 Videotape Depositions

Videotape depositions are being used with increasing frequency. These depositions may be taken by the attorney who retained you with the intent of playing them at trial in lieu of the appearance of the deponent live. (The other attorneys would be afforded the opportunity to cross-examine you at the deposition.) A major advantage of videotape depositions of expert witnesses is that these may save the parties the expense of having to pay an expert to testify twice in a case— once at deposition and once at trial. To excel during videotape depositions, you will need to know more about them.

Research has shown that videotaped depositions are more revealing and have a much more dramatic impact than reading into the record traditional stenographically recorded depositions. (Stenographically recorded depositions may be permitted as a way of getting the testimony of a witness into evidence without having that witness testify live in court.) Videotaped depositions permit the jury or fact finder to better evaluate the credibility of the expert witness.

> Taking a deposition by visual means such as videotape is advantageous if the deposition is introduced at trial, because the fact finder at the trial often will gain greater insight from the manner in which an answer is delivered and recorded by audiovisual devices and will avoid the tedium that is produced when counsel reads lengthy depositions into evidence at the trial. A videotaped deposition

provides the best means for the court and the jury to judge the demeanor of the witness....[1]

In the television age, jurors are conditioned to watch, listen, believe, and in many cases, remember what they see on the screen.

> Jurors are more likely to be influenced by a video presentation than a deposition transcript. Jurors remember what they see and hear more than what they merely read. Videotape tends to capture and hold the attention of a jury. A deposition transcript, by contrast, can be quite boring. Jurors who are used to television as a medium of communication tend to be comfortable with the presence of a television screen in the courtroom.[2]

Videotape depositions also provide better ammunition for impeachment if the deponent does testify at trial because the cross-examiner can play the video of the allegedly inconsistent statement. Videotape depositions usually result in less coaching by counsel as well because the camera (and jury) can pick up on such techniques.

8.1 Rules and Procedures

Federal Rule of Civil Procedure 30(b)(4) provides:

> Unless otherwise agreed by the parties, a deposition shall be conducted before an officer appointed or designated under Rule 28 and shall begin with a statement on the record by the officer that includes

---

[1] 10 Fed. Proc. L.Ed., p. 657

[2] Paul Michael Lisneck and Michael J. Kaufman, *Depositions: Procedures, Strategy, and Technique* (St Paul, MN: West Publishing, 1995) 7-11.

(A) the officer's name and business address; (B) the
date, time, and place of the deposition; (C) the name
of the deponent; (D) the administration of the oath or
affirmation to the deponent; and (E) an identification
of all persons present. If the deposition is recorded
other than stenographically, the officer shall repeat
items (A) through (C) at the beginning of each unit
of recorded tape or other recording medium. The
appearance or demeanor of deponents or attorneys
shall not be distorted through camera or sound-
recording techniques. At the end of the deposition,
the officer shall state on the record that the
deposition is complete and shall set forth any
stipulations made by counsel concerning the custody
of the transcript or recording and the exhibits, or
concerning other pertinent matters.

Rule 30(b)(4) provides only general parameters
on what cannot be done. The distortion of the
appearance or demeanor of a deponent through camera
or sound recording techniques is the only specific
prohibition. The 1993 amendments to 30(b)(4)
encouraged increased use of videotaped depositions by
no longer requiring counsel to obtain permission of the
court or agreement from other counsel before
videotaping a deposition.

NOTICE

FRCP 30(b)(2) requires that the deposition notice
specify if it is going to be videotaped:

> (2) The party taking the deposition shall state in the
> notice the method by which the testimony shall be
> recorded....

You should review the deposition notice
carefully to see if the testimony is going to be

videotaped. If the deposition is going to be used as evidence at trial in lieu of live oral testimony, the notice should state this.

8.2 Looking Good for the Camera

The videotape of your deposition may ultimately be played to the jury. It is important, therefore, that you make a good impression on camera. Normally, you will rely on counsel for the party who has retained you to insure that the taping is done fairly, impartially, and without operator bias or distortion. Nevertheless, to avoid disaster and professional embarrassment, you should have at least a basic understanding of the technical aspects of the taping.

CAMERA SHOTS AND ANGLES

Gregory P. Joseph notes in *ALI-ABA's Practice Checklist Manual on Taking Depositions* that there are four basic camera shots used in depositions.

- The full or establishing shot, which is a wide-angle view which establishes the scene showing all participants;
- The two-shot, which includes head and shoulders of two people, the deponent and the examining attorney;
- The medium shot, which includes only the head and shoulders of the deponent; and
- The close-up, which is a tight shot which focuses on an exhibit or a limited area of an individual's body, such as the head.[3]

---

[3] Gregory P. Joseph, *ALI-ABA's Practice Checklist Manual on Taking Depositions* (Philadelphia, PA: American Law Institute) 92.

The four basic moves of the camera are:

- zooming (closing in),
- panning (moving the camera horizontally),
- tilting, and
- trucking or dollying (moving the entire camera).

LAWYER TACTICS

Despite the admonition in the Rules against distortion of the appearance or demeanor of the witness, tactical advantages may be sought by counsel. Techniques used by counsel at videotape deposition may include the following.

1. Pacing to force the experts' eyes to move back and forth. This makes the expert look "shifty."
2. Pointing the camera up at the expert to make him or her look sinister.
3. Lighting to wash out the witness or placing the expert in shadows.
4. Using an extreme close-up to make the expert look harsh and to emphasize facial expressions and movements.
5. Getting the expert angry or upset so the jury or fact finder can see his or her "true nature."

Unfortunately, there is little you can do to prevent these actions by counsel. It will be up to counsel that retained you to make sure that your image is not distorted.

8.3 Use of Videotape Depositions for Impeachment

It is important to understand and remember that a videotaped deposition may be used to later cross-examine and impeach you if you appear as a witness at trial. [See *Warner v. General Motors Corp.* 357 N.W.2d 689 (1984).] Prior to being impeached by a videotape deposition at trial, you need *not* be afforded any advance notice or warning by counsel. Because the tape of the deposition can be used against you during trial, you must try to excel when giving your videotape deposition. Rule 613 of the Federal Rules of Evidence governs and is printed below.

Fed. R. Evid. 613 Prior Statements of Witnesses (a) Examining witness concerning prior statement. In examining a witness concerning a prior statement made by the witness, whether written or not, the statement need not be shown nor its contents disclosed to the witness at that time, but on request the same shall be shown or disclosed to opposing counsel.

In litigation involving expert witnesses and a lot of money, lawyers are making more and more sophisticated use of videotaped depositions. With the permission of the trial judge, they can edit and compress the testimony of the expert to compare and contrast it with live testimony and even documents and other exhibits. The impact can be devastating. Consider this example used during the tobacco litigation of 1998.

> FTI, one of a number of consultants that advise lawyers on trial technology, specializes in such techniques as putting someone's image alongside a

smoking-gun document and freezing the film on a phrase or facial expression.

The firm recently digitized more than 600 hours of videotaped testimony for Mr. Bartlit for a trial. As a result, any fragment could be called up within seconds by typing a page number of the written transcript into a laptop computer.

Videos can help lawyers underscore points. In Minnesota's landmark trial against the tobacco industry to recover the health-care costs of treating sick smokers, which settled earlier this year, the state played a large portion of a deposition of Philip Morris Co's. former research director, Thomas Osdene, invoking his Fifth Amendment protection against self-incrimination 135 times.[4]

8.4 How to Excel During Videotape Depositions

It is especially important to excel during your videotape deposition. This videotape could be the only means by which the jury receives your testimony. You will need to look and sound good. If you do testify at trial, your videotape deposition may be used at trial to impeach you. The authors recommend the following.

1. Prepare with counsel and practice before a videotape camera. Upon reviewing the tape, you should be able to note your annoying, distracting, or unfavorable mannerisms, methods of answering questions, or nervous habits. Correction of these mannerisms can make the difference between an expert who appears nervous and anxious to the jury and

---

[4] "In Videotape Depositions, Every Twitch Tells a Tale," *Wall Street Journal Legal Beat,* 12/8/98, B1.

one who is calm, collected, and professional.[5]

2. Dress conservatively. Do not appear with gaudy or flashy jewelry, cell phones, or pagers. Image is extremely important. You don't want to turn the jury off or lose credibility.

3. Men should try and get a close shave prior to the deposition. You'll look better on camera if you do.

4. Look directly at the camera when testifying. You will keep the jury more interested and appear more credible.

5. Avoid long, pregnant pauses that may make you look evasive or uninformed.

6. When handling exhibits, make sure you hold them so that they can be appreciated fully by the viewers. To avoid glare, turn off view boxes when not in use.

7. Avoid eating, smoking, drinking, chewing gum, or chewing on pens or pencils. This may distract the jury, make you look bad, and may make the audio portion of your testimony harder to understand. If the jury is distracted or has to listen closely to understand you, it is likely that they will daydream and not listen to you at all.

8. Turn off pagers, cell phones, and beepers and do not take phone calls. You want to appear as though your entire focus is on the questioning and that you are taking your responsibility seriously. If you don't focus on your testimony, why should the jury?

---

[5] Be aware though, that this preparation session can be a subject of inquiry at the deposition. "Did you meet with counsel prior to giving this deposition today...? What did you do and discuss?"

Chapter 9 Handling Abuse

You may be exposed to various levels of abuse when you are giving an expert deposition. This abuse may come in several different forms, including abusive questioning, nonpayment of your fee, and wasting your time.

9.1 Abusive Questioning

The American legal system is an adversary system. This means, in part, that parties to a dispute are allowed to cross-examine witnesses aggressively in an attempt to determine the truth. As an expert witness, you can expect to be examined aggressively. Most of this aggressive questioning will be appropriate, legal, and ethical. *If you are thin skinned and do not want to subject yourself to aggressive questioning, your best course of action may be to choose not to involve yourself in the case as an expert witness.*

Expert witnesses who testify at deposition must be prepared to deal with occasional abusive questioning by counsel. The expert who understands his legal rights and remedies is in the strongest position to deal with abuse. However, aggressive examination is generally allowed. FRCP 30(d)3 deals with what is not allowed.

> **Fed. R. Civ. Pro. 30(d)3**
> At any time during a deposition, on motion of a party or of the deponent and upon a showing that the examination is being conducted in bad faith or in such manner as unreasonably to annoy, embarrass, or oppress the deponent or party, the court in which the action is pending or the court in the district where the deposition is being taken may order the officer conducting the examination to cease forthwith from taking the deposition, or may limit the scope and manner of the taking of the deposition as provided in Rule 26(c).

The expert witness, therefore, has the right under the Federal Rules to seek protection from the judge overseeing the case. A request for a protective order can be sought by the expert, his or her counsel, or by counsel for the party who has retained the expert.

What kind of abusive questions can expert witnesses anticipate and how far is too far? Abusive types of questioning include: repetitive lengthy questioning, vulgarity, hostility, personal attacks, and demeaning and sarcastic remarks by counsel. How far is too far would ultimately have to be decided by a judge. The judge would need to make a factual determination that the deposition is "being conducted in bad faith, or in such manner as unreasonably to annoy, embarrass, or oppress the deponent."[1] When an attorney crosses the line, you may know it right away.[2] If you terminate a deposition without substantial justification, you may become liable for sanctions. You therefore want to be sure that an attorney has definitely

---

[1] Fed. R. Civ. Pro. 30(d)(3).
[2] E.g., "This piece of fucking shit you call a report, did Attorney Jones tell you what to write in it?"

crossed the line before you suspend the deposition unilaterally.

REPETITIVE QUESTIONS

It may be annoying for counsel to repeatedly and deliberately ask the same questions over and over again. This tactic is designed to trip up the expert by obtaining different responses and getting the expert upset. In most cases, counsel will be granted substantial leeway by a judge regarding repetitive questions. Thus, the most appropriate way for the expert to respond is by simply answering the questions.

Remember that you are being compensated for your time. You should, therefore, exercise tireless patience and politeness. Once counsel realizes that he is getting the same answer over and over again and that you will not become flustered, he will move on.

In many instances, counsel for the party who has retained you will interject an objection because she is losing her patience. Let counsel argue amongst themselves. If they want you to answer the question, answer it and force counsel to move on.

Example 9.1
Q: Why did you join the American Society of Agricultural Engineers?
A: I have already answered that question. How much more of this do I have to take?... You know I do have other things to do besides sit here and answer your inane questions.

Lesson: Counsel has obtained the desired result—he has gotten the expert flustered and upset. If the expert does not calm down quickly, he will be less effective in answering additional questions. Furthermore, in videotape depositions, these flashes of anger may put off the jury or fact finder. A better answer might have been, "To obtain their newsletter and publications."

HOSTILITY

Expert witnesses may be faced with many hostile questions at deposition. The best way to deal with these questions is to maintain your demeanor and simply answer the questions. Remember that counsel is frequently role playing with his or her display of hostility. A calm and collected answer will make the lawyer look like a bully and should bolster your credibility. If the question is so blatantly personal, hostile, or vulgar that you in no way can dignify it with a response, suspend the deposition and consult an attorney immediately.[3] Otherwise, answer the question in a calm, professional manner and force counsel to move on.

Example 9.2
Q: When you do a medical/legal examination for someone, like this insurance company, it doesn't matter if the claimant gets better or takes their medication, does it? Because all you care about is doing the exams, and satisfying your client, and getting more medical/legal work in the future, isn't that correct?

Lesson: The best way to deal with this question is to simply answer it "No."

---

[3] E.g., "You're nothing but a fucking whore for the insurance companies, aren't you?"

PERSONAL ATTACKS: DEMEANING AND SARCASTIC REMARKS

Some lawyers taking depositions go too far with personal attacks and sarcastic and demeaning remarks. The clearest examples of such questioning would be sexist comments, racial or ethnic slurs, vulgarity, or other clearly inappropriate comments. Experts need not take this type of abuse at deposition. Counsel should be given a warning "to make a record." For example, you might state on the record, "I will have no choice but to terminate this deposition. This is your final warning." If the improper conduct persists, you should terminate the deposition and *immediately* consult an attorney.

Example 9.3
Q: You testified that you obtained your degree in India. Did they have an accredited medical school there or was it instruction mainly for medicine men?

Q: Your hobbies listed on your CV are bird watching and dancing.... What about home decorating? Do you do any of that, as well, sir?

Lesson: In the authors' opinion, a judge would probably find that these questions have crossed the line. The expert should warn counsel on the record. If the personal abuse continues and you do not want to take any more, terminate the deposition and consult an attorney immediately.

If the warning does not work, the expert may need to terminate the deposition and seek a protective order.

If the opposing attorney is hostile or uses intimidating questions and tactics, he should be cautioned on the record, and if the deposition is not being videotaped, the party cautioning the abusive attorney should clearly state on the record what it is that is being objected to and make repeated nonantagonistic requests that the abusive conduct be ceased. After making as clear a record as possible, clearly inform the abusive attorney that you will seek judicial protection if the activity continues.[4]

Counsel who go too far may be subject to legal action. For example, in the case of *Florida Bar v. Schaub* 618 So.2d 202 (Fla.1993), a prosecutor was suspended for thirty days after he insulted a defense expert, elicited irrelevant information from the expert, and expressed his own derogatory opinions of the expert's field.

The key to success for an expert who is faced with abusive questioning is when to start to push back. The test of how much counsel can get away with is one of reasonableness.

The deponent has no redress unless the annoyance, embarrassment, or oppression will be unreasonable, and the seeking of information is not unreasonably annoying, embarrassing, or oppressive if the information is material and relevant.[5]

Remember that as a witness in a case your credibility is a major issue. Thus, questions about licensing, criminal convictions, fees earned, suspensions, exclusion of prior testimony, prior expert

---

[4] James L. Branton and Jim D. Lovett, *Depositions* (Ft. Worth, TX: Knowles Publishing, Inc., 1998) 28.
[5] *Federal Procedure,* Lawyer's Edition (Rochester, NY: Lawyers' Cooperative Publishing, 1994) 654.

witnessing work, etc. are all fair game and should be answered without hesitation. If you do not want to be subjected to such questioning, you should choose not to involve yourself in the case as an expert witness.

Example 9.4

Q: Did you flunk the exam for certification three times before you finally passed it, sir?
A: Yes.
Q: You were convicted of tax evasion in 1997, correct?
A: Yes.
Q: You have earned over $1.5 million in performing IME exams in the last ten years, correct?
A: That's correct.
Q: Your license was suspended for how many years starting in 1991?
A: Two years.
Q: Your testimony on hedonic damages was excluded in six different cases, correct?
A: That's correct.
Q: According to your CV, you have testified over 500 times in depositions in court, correct?
A: Yes.

Lesson: As an expert witness, your credibility is a legitimate and important issue in a case. All of the above questions and answers may be embarrassing and annoying, but they are permissible because they relate to your credibility.

9.2 Nonpayment of Fees

This is an abuse that all expert witnesses may experience at one time or another. As an expert witness, you are entitled to be compensated for your time at a deposition. The best policy is to ask for payment well in advance of giving the deposition. Most attorneys will comply with this request and it will obviate the problem of collecting your fee.

If you have not collected your fee up front, you should bill the person or entity responsible for paying your fee immediately after the deposition. If the bill is not paid, call and ask that it be paid. Do not let the attorney browbeat you into waiting for payment or accept his or her excuses (which may often happen). If the bill is not paid, you may threaten or file legal action. If the party responsible for your bill is the party that retained you, you can consider refusing to do further work on the case until your outstanding bills are paid.

9.3 Wasted Time

During depositions, there are three ways that the time of expert witnesses is frequently wasted. First, experts may be asked a seemingly endless series of repetitive questions. Second, a deposition may be cancelled on short notice and the expert may lose the profitable use of the blocked-out time. Third, the expert may be called upon to conduct lengthy and wasteful travel.

The authors recommend three simple solutions to these problems. First, charge by the hour. You are very likely to be taken advantage of through lengthy questioning if you charge a flat fee for a deposition. Second, insist up front on a nonrefundable deposit for the late cancellation of your deposition. This is easily justified because late cancellations can be very costly to you. Finally, ask for an agreement up front to bill for your travel time portal to portal. Counsel is not likely to ask you to drive all over the state if she is paying you $350 per hour for your travel time.[6]

[6] See, e.g., *Haarhuis v. Kunnan Enterprises, Ltd.*, 223 B.R. 252 (D.D.C. 1998). (The expert was entitled to be paid $300 per hour portal to portal for travel time from his office in Baltimore, MD, to Washington, DC. The deposing party insisted the deposition take place in Washington rather than at the deponent expert's office in Baltimore.)

Appendix A Deposition Checklist

Expert witnesses who are thoroughly prepared will excel at deposition. A brief checklist that may be helpful follows. You may want to use this as a quick mental checklist. *__Caveat:__ The use of this checklist and any other methods for your preparation may be legitimate areas of inquiry at deposition. If you use a written checklist, that may have to be produced in response to a subpoena duces tecum.*

Deposition Checklist for Experts

—Adequate time set aside for deposition and travel
—Appearance and grooming
      —Clothes set aside
—Bias
      —Likely questions on bias
—Compensation
      —Fees by client to date
      —Hourly rate
      —Who is responsible for paying for deposition?
      —Amount for deposition
      —Has payment been received in advance for deposition?
—Conference with counsel
      —Date and time
      —Likely areas of inquiry
—Curriculum vitae
      —Is CV up to date?
      —Is CV completely accurate?
—Dates
      —When were you first contacted by counsel?
      —Method of contact?
      —Case accepted when?

—Records received when?
—When were your opinions formed?
—When did you write reports (if any)?
—Discovery reviewed to date
  —Complaint
  —Answers to interrogatories
  —Depositions
—Drawing at deposition
  —What is likely to be requested?
—Facts mastered?
  —Brief summary of facts, important names, dates, and locations
—Location of deposition
—Noted on calendar?
—Opinions
  —Assumptions made
  —Clinical methodology used
  —Equipment used
  —Factual basis for opinion
  —Reports or documents relied on
  —Testing performed
  —What will you offer opinions on?
  —What areas will you not offer opinions on?
  —When were your opinions formed?
—Photographs, reports and test results in your possession
—Prior sworn testimony in previous cases involving the same/similar issue
—Reports
  —Oral
  —Preliminary
  —Final
—Subpoena duces tecum
  —Received?
  —What are you required to produce?
  —Is the requested material in your file?

—Waive reading and signing?
—Writings
    —Past writings available to impeach you?
    —Authoritative writings?

Appendix B Sample Answers to Interrogatories

COMMONWEALTH OF MASSACHUSETTS
NORFOLK, SS.

SUPERIOR COURT DEPARTMENT
CIVIL ACTION NO. 90-00447

****

CHARLES SMITH; PATRICIA	*
SMITH; and KATELYN SMITH,	*
KYLE SMITH, and MATTHEW	*
SMITH, Minors by Their	*
Mother and Next Friend,	*
PATRICIA SMITH,	*
PLAINTIFF, CHARLES SMITH'S	*
Plaintiffs	*
	*
VS.	*
	*
ABC CONSTRUCTION CO., INC.,	*
Defendant	*

****

PLAINTIFF'S ANSWERS TO DEFENDANT'S
INTEROGATORRIES

Q. 1. Please identify yourself by stating your full
name, date of birth, social security number, residence,
employer, business address, occupation and, if married,
the name of your spouse.

A. 1. Charles Smith; 4/6/48; 039-28-59 ʒ5; 27 Harbor
Road, Jackson, RI; Unemployed; Not applicable;
Framing Carpenter/Disabled; Patricia Smith.

Q. 2. Please describe in full detail how the alleged accident occurred, stating what you saw, heard, did and what happened to you in order in which the events took place.

A. 2. We returned to the job site at 10 Maple Drive in Wilder, Massachusetts, on the morning of February 24, 1988. I went over to the area of the cellar hole opening that we had covered with plywood laid down on framing timbers and I saw it had been covered over with plastic since we were there the previous week. I went over to remove the plastic sheet and I stepped on the plywood covering the hole. When I stepped on the plywood my foot went through and I fell 3 feet or so when I got hung up on a steel center beam which was below the opening. I came down on to this steel beam with my back and my right shoulder making contact.

Q. 3. Please state the exact hour, day and date and when the alleged accident occurred.

A. 3. The accident occurred on February 24, 1988, at about 7:00 A.M.

Q. 4. Please give a complete description of the injuries you received as a result of the alleged accident.

A. 4. As a result of this accident I suffered herniated disc in my lower back with right leg pains resulting from the sciatic nerve. This has been diagnosed as herniated nucleus pulposis at L5-S1, with sciatica.

Q. 5. Please give a complete description of the injuries which you believe to be permanent as a result of the alleged accident.

A. 5. I believe the injury of herniated disc with residual back pain and sciatic pain as described in answer to question 4 permanent. I have suffered symptoms continuously from the date of the accident through the present by reason of such injuries.

Q. 6. If, as a result of any injuries received with regard to this alleged accident, you received medical and/or other treatment, state:

a. The name and address of any and all persons or institutions from which you received such medical or other treatment;

b. The number of treatments so received, setting forth as accurately as possible, all dates of treatment and a description of said treatments;

c. The number and description of treatments received at a doctor's office or institution and the number at your home; and

d. An itemized account of all expenses incurred for the above referred to treatments.

A. 6. My medical treatment has included the following:

<u>V.A. Hospital</u>
Epworth, RI

2/25/88	Orthopedic Clinic, X-ray $127.00
3/1/88	Orthopedic Clinic $127.00

4/20/88	Orthopedic Clinic
	$127.00
5/4/88	Orthopedic Clinic, X-ray
	$127.00
6/29/88	Orthopedic Clinic
	$127.00
7/5-7/8/88	Inpatient: CT and Myelogram
	$1,419.00
7/27/88	Orthopedic Clinic
	$127.00
8/22-8/26/88	Inpatient Care
	$1,892.00
8/29-9/3/88	Inpatient: Disc Surgery
	$3,055.00
9/19/88	Orthopedic Follow-up
	$127.00
10/17/88	Orthopedic Clinic
	$110.00
11/28/88	Orthopedic Clinic
	$110.00
12/5-12/10/88	Inpatient: CAT Scan, Myelogram
	$2,415.00
8/14/89	Orthopedic Clinic
	$110.00
10/4/89	Orthopedic Clinic
	$116.00
10/6/89	Physical Therapy
	$116.00
10/11/89	Physical Therapy
	$116.00
10/16/89	Physical Therapy
	$116.00
10/20/89	Physical Therapy
	$116.00
10/23/89	Physical Therapy
	$116.00

10/25/89	Physical Therapy
	$116.00
11/1/89	Physical Therapy
	$116.00
11/3/89	Physical Therapy
	$116.00
1/11/90	Orthopedic Clinic, X-ray
	$116.00
4/4/90	Orthopedic Clinic
	$116.00
4/10/90	Physical Therapy
	$116.00
10/23/90	Orthopedic Clinic
	$116.00

More detailed information is contained on my medical records, copies of which are being provided to Defendant in response to request for production of documents.

Q. 7. a. Please state the dates between which you were confined to your home as a result of the alleged accident;

b. Please state the dates between which you were confined to your bed as a result;

c. Please state the dates between which you were absent from work as a result of the alleged accident.

A. 7. a. After seeing the doctor on February 25, 1988, I went home and stayed home for one week. On March 1, 1988, I went out again, to see the doctor.

Following this visit, I went back to work for a period of weeks between March 5, 1988, and April 15, 1988. I worked only a few days each week, and I missed many days due to back pain. I did not keep a record of these days. I last worked on April 15, 1988. On those days that I missed, I was confined to home, at bed rest.

After seeing the doctor on April 20, 1988, I stayed home at bed rest for 2 weeks, and I have remained at home since that time. Gradually, I have increased my ability to get out of the house, to where I now can be up and about from one to two hours per day. The remainder of the time, I am still confined to home, with frequent bed rest.

b. I was confined to bed, at home from February 25, 1988, after seeing the doctor, to March 3, 1988. I was confined to bed at home, on doctor's orders, from April 20, 1988, through May 3, 1988. I was confined to bed, in hospital, from July 5, 188, to July 8, 1988. I was confined to bed at home from July 9, 1988, to July 27, 1988, when I returned to the doctor. I remained at bedrest, at home, from July 28, 1988, to August 21, 1988. I remained at bedrest, in hospital, from August 22, 1988, to August 26, 1988, to August 28, 1988. I remained at bedrest, in hospital, from August 29, 1988, through September 3, 1988. I remained at bedrest, at home, from September 4, 1988, to September 19, 1988, when I returned to the doctor. I remained at bedrest, at home, from September 20, 1988, to October 17, 1988, when I returned to the doctor. I remained at bedrest at home, on doctor's orders, from October 18, 1988, to November 28, 1988, when I saw the doctor again. I was confined to bedrest, in hospital, from December 5, 1988, through December 10, 1988.

At all other times, from and after April 20, 1988, I have remained sedentary, spending most of my time at home sitting or reclining, with gradual increase in my ability to get up and about.

c. I have been out of work, as follows:

February 25, 1988, through March 4, 1988; and April 18, 1988, to present.

Also, I missed several days between March 5, 1988, and April 15, 1988, but I have no record of these days.

Q. 8. Describe fully and in complete detail any illnesses, injuries, diseases, defects or operations which you may have or suffered from:

a. within five years prior to the date of the alleged accident;

b. at any time subsequent to the date of the alleged accident; and

c. at any time after the date of the alleged accident not caused by or arising from the same, setting forth the dates upon which each of the above was had or suffered from.

A. 8. a. With the exception of the occasional cold or flu, I had no illness, injuries, diseases, defects or operations within 5 years prior to February 24, 1988. In 1969, while serving in Vietnam, I injured my back, and since that time, over the years, I did experience occasional backaches, for which I was treated at the VA Hospital Orthopedic Clinic. Also, in 1987 or 1988, I experienced some ankle swelling, but I do not know of any accident or injury that caused the swelling.

b. With the exception only of the occasional cold or flu, and the residual affects and/or treatment for the injury I sustained on February 24, 1988, I have had no further illness, injuries, diseases, defects or operations since that time.

c. With the exception only of the occasional cold or flu, and the residual affects and/or treatment for the injury I sustained on February 24, 1988, I have had no further illness, injuries, diseases, defects or operations since that time.

Q. 9. State the name and residence, business address, occupation, and specialty of each person you expect may be called by you as an expert witness at the trial of this action, setting forth:

a. the subject matter in detail on which each such person may be expected to testify;

b. in detail, the substance of all facts about which each such person may be expected to testify; and

c. in detail, the contents of all opinions to which each such person may be expected to testify.

A. 9. <u>Patrick McDonald, M.D.</u>
15 Kildeer Blvd.
Providence, RI 02907

(a) Dr. McDonald will be asked to testify as to Charles Smith's injuries, including diagnosis, causation, prognosis, symptomology, loss of function and disability.

(b) Dr. McDonald will testify as to the following facts and opinions.

REPORTED HISTORY: The patient is a 42-year-old male who had been employed for three and a half years of Acme Construction as a carpenter prior to his injury. The injury occurred on February 24, 1988 at about 10:00 A.M. He fell through an opening in the floor, falling about four feet and landing diagonally across a metal beam. He struck his lower back and injured his upper back and shoulder as well. He was able with some difficulty to sit and wait out the rest of the day. He did very little work. Since it was a Friday, he went home.

The following Monday because of increasing pain, he was seen at the VA Hospital. He was evaluated over a period of months. He did not improve and, in fact, he began developing right leg pain for which he underwent a lumbar laminectory by Dr. Lynne in August of 1988. He says the numbness and some of the pain in his right leg improved briefly after that but then his low back pain became more severe and his right leg pain returned. He is now using crutches for stability. He has physical therapy ongoing three times a week and he sees the VA people back about every three months.

Current Complaints: He has basically pain which is quite extreme in his low back, into both groins and into his right leg down to the ankle. He denies any pain on the left side. He is able to drive a car but does so only rarely. He is anxious to try and get better but is also concerned that another operation may not help him any more than the first.

PAST MEDICAL HISTORY: Medications: Percocet, Tylenol No. 3 and Motrin. Medical problems: None. He smokes one half pack of cigarettes a day for 20 years. He admits to no alcohol use. Surgical history is for tonsils and adenoids and lumbar laminectomy.

PHYSICAL EXAMINATION: On examination, he is 6'1" tall and weighs 230 pounds. He is able to move with an antalgic gait around the room. There seems to be some weakness on dorsiflexion on the right side compared to the left. His EHL on the right is slightly weak as well. His reflexes are 1+ Achilles tendon and patella tendon. Straight-leg raising sitting is negative on the left side to about 60 degrees.

On the right side, it is positive at about 40 degrees sitting with pain down the right lower extremity below the knee. When he is recumbent, I can get the right leg only up to about 20 degrees before again he has right radicular type of pain. On the left side, I can get it to about 40 degrees before he has significant low back pain. He has a well-healed incision in the lumbar spine which is about two inches in length which is minimally tender to palpation. SI joints are slightly tender but the sciatic notch on the right is exquisitely tender compared to the left side.

Forward bending of the lumbar spine is perhaps 20 degrees at best, and extension is neutral. Lateral flexion is about 3 degrees at best and rotation is really not possible.

DIAGNOSIS: Status-post herniated lumbar disc with chronic low back pain and radicular pain, right lower extremity, suggestive of recurrent disc.

ASSESSMENT: It is Dr. McDonald's opinion that the patient's injury occurred acutely as a result of his job on February 24, 1988.

Based on examination of 6/22/90, it is Dr. McDonald's opinion that Plaintiff is not capable of returning to his regular work. He is capable of minimal sedentary work.

Dr. McDonald concurs with the need for aggressive therapy, also for the evaluation for facet blocks and work up to see if the patient has indeed another fragment of disc where he is in need of further surgery would be appropriate as well.

Dr. Danes would concur that there is a functional overlay here which is almost expected given a two year history of out of work with significant back injury.

(c) The bases of Dr. McDonald's opinions include the history taken from Plaintiff and the observations made during examination on June 22, 1990.

Steven Danes, M.D.

(a) Dr. Danes will be asked to testify as to Charles Smith's injuries, including diagnosis, causation, prognosis, symptomology, loss of function and disability.

(b) Dr. Danes will testify as to the following facts and opinion:

REPORTED HISTORY: The patient was seen on November 3, 1988, and on January 23, 1990. Patient is 41-year-old male who worked as a framing carpenter for ACME Construction for about two and a half years.

He sustained an injury to his low back on February 24, 1988, when he was on the deck of a building and walked onto a piece of plywood covering a fireplace opening which gave way. He fell approximately two feet backwards and his back hit a steel center beam. He was unable to hold himself from fall further by grabbing the beam.

He was initially seen at the Veterans Administration Hospital and was subsequently seen in the orthopedic clinic there by Dr. Lynne. He underwent lumbar spine surgery on August 31, 1988. Post-operatively, he states that he continued to have symptoms.

Interval History: The patient states that his right leg numbness and deadness have resolved approximately 90 percent. However, he continues to have severe low back pain and some difficulty with the right lower extremity. He has been to physical therapy for about two weeks but could not tolerate the therapeutic regimen.

Complaints are of persistent severe pain in the low back with difficulty moving at all out of a recliner chair or bed. He states that he spends most of his day lying or sitting in a recliner chair or in his bed and has used two crutches for ambulation, having progressed to two canes, and having the feeling of instability and increasing back pain. He takes two Percocet every six hours, 800 milligrams of Ibuprofen every six hours and two Soma tablets every six to eight hours.

Post-operatively, the patient did undergo a myelogram and CT Scan. He remains under the care of Dr. Lynne. A second operation is under consideration.

PAST HISTORY: The patient denies any interval injury since last seen or since his injury of February 24, 1988. Past history is positive for some low back pain with his work. He never had leg pain or missed any work because of this.

PHYSICAL EXAMINATION: Height is 6'1" tall and weight is 235 pounds. Patient enters the building and the exam room with two crutches and a very slow and cautious gait, limping on the right lower extremity. He has a two inch mid-line lumbar scar and tenderness over the scar.

There is no paraspinous spasm although he does withdraw on palpation of his scar. Lumbar range of motion is quite limited with 30 degrees of flexion, 15 degrees of left and right side bending and 5 degrees of extension. Deep-tendon reflexes are trace at the knees bilaterally and absent at the right ankle and trace at the left ankle. Sensation is preserved to light touch in the lower extremities. Motor testing shows 5/5 strength of extensor hallucis longus, tibialis anterior and quadriceps bilaterally.

The sciatic stretch tests on the right in the seated position is positive for his radiating pain as well as in the supine position. However, the sciatic stretch test is aggravated by knee flexion. Also of note is a positive patella tilt sign with complaints of low back pain aggravation by manipulation of the right patella. This is indicative of significant non-anatomic pain. He also has a slightly positive axial compression test.

DIAGNOSIS: Severe back pain and status post failed lumbar disc surgery.

ASSESSMENT: The onset of this patient's problem was the injury at work as stated above.

A subsequent course and failure to improve stems from that original injury.

The patient does show objective signs of limitation of lumbar motion and decreased right ankle jerk. He is not capable of regular or light work at this time.

In addition, he shows significant overlay of psychophysiological pain experienced as demonstrated by exacerbation of his pain by knee flexion and patella tilt sign.

Prognosis is extremely guarded given his progress to date.

(c) The bases of Dr. Danes's opinions include the history taken from Plaintiff and the observations made during examinations on November 3, 1988, and January 23, 1990.

Q. 10. State whether or not there were any witnesses to the alleged accident and, if so, state the name and address of all such witnesses other than the parties involved in this suit.

A. 10. Yes, there were witnesses present. They include:

John Williams, 900 Correy Street, Pawtucket, RI.
Karl Amons , 416 Kaspar Lane, Pawtucket, RI.
Thomas Andrews, 40 W. School Rd., Pawtucket, RI.

Q. 11. State what, if any, you consumed by way of any alcoholic beverages or drugs for a period of 24 hours prior to this accident, setting forth in detail where same were consumed, the type of alcohol or drugs, the amounts thereof consumed by you, and at what time intervals.

A. 11. I had no alcohol nor any medications or drugs within 24 hours prior to this accident.

Q. 12. Give an itemized statement of all monetary loss sustained by you as a result of the alleged accident.

A. 12. My economic loss to date is as follows:

Medical Expense:

V.A. Hospital
2/25/88 to present
As itemized at No. 6, above:
$11,506.00

Lost Earning Capacity:

Total disability from 4/15/88 to present,
$57,640.00
131 weeks at $440

Both medical expense and lost earning capacity continue to accrue, and these sums are expected to increase accordingly through the date of trial.

Q. 13. Please state in detail and as fully as possible, all conversations or the substance thereof that any defendant had with you or others in your presence concerning the alleged accident, stating as accurately as you are able, what was said by each.

A. 13. I do not recall any conversations with ABC Construction Company, Inc. Nor do I recall any conversations with ABC's owner, individually.

Q. 14. State with reference to the time of the alleged accident, the occupation in which you were engaged, setting forth the name of your employer, the particular capacity in which you were employed, and the wages, salary or profit you were receiving at that time.

A. 14. At the time of this accident I was employed by ACME Construction Company Inc. I was employed as a framing carpenter. I was earning $11.00 an hour, and I was averaging 40 hours a week.

Q. 15. If as a result of this accident you have received compensation from workers' compensation or other insurer, please identify the insurer and state the amounts received on a weekly basis and/or lump sum basis.

A. 15.
a. Workers' Compensation, Goode Insurance Co. $213.84 per week.

b. Other insurance
Social Security Disability, Title II
$171 per month
Q. 16. If you allege that the occurrence resulted in whole or in part from a defective condition involving the defendant's equipment or premises, please:

a. describe the alleged defective condition in complete detail;

b. state how long to your knowledge the alleged defective condition had existed prior to the alleged occurrence;

c. state whether or not you had observed or otherwise become aware of the alleged defective condition prior to the alleged occurrence.

A. 16. a. The defective condition consisted of a makeshift covering over the floor hole which was not properly secured by nailing and/or cross bracing. This consisted solely of half inch plywood laid across the opening. There were two sheets of plywood which were laid side-by-side over the hole and were not lapped over each other. This plywood was not adequate to support the weight of a 210-pound adult male. Additionally, the plywood was covered by plastic sheeting which obscured the edges of the plywood where it lapped over the perimeter of the hole, so I could not see that the 2x4 cross bracing had been removed.

b. The condition existed at least 24–48 hours to the best of my knowledge and information.

c. No. I was unaware of the defective condition prior to the accident. I was aware that when the ACME crew for whom I was working left the job site approximately one week earlier, we left the floor opening properly covered by laying 2x4's on the flat across the floor opening and then covering it with half-inch plywood which was nailed through to the decking.

Q. 17. Please give the date and time of day when you first saw the defect or defective condition in existence.

A. 17. I first became aware of the defective condition when my foot went through and I fell into the hole.

Q. 18. If you claim that the negligence of any person or persons, including the defendant, contributed to cause the alleged occurrence, please state their names and the manner in which each contributed to cause the alleged occurrence.

A. 18. The negligence of ABC Construction Co., Inc. (Defendant) arose in two contexts:

(a) as owner and party in control of the premises at 10 Maple Drive, Wilder, MA; and

(b) as general contractor, in charge of all construction activities at that location.

The specific negligent conduct of Defendant included:

(a) as owner or party in control of the premises, Defendant was negligent in failing to maintain the premises in a reasonably safe condition for lawful visitors by creating or permitting to exist an unreasonably dangerous and defective condition: i.e., an inadequately and improperly covered floor opening on the premises.

(b) as general contractor, Defendant was negligent in creating or permitting to exist on premises under construction an unreasonably dangerous and defective condition: i.e., an inadequately and improperly covered floor opening.

Also, as general contractor, Defendant failed to warn of the dangerous and defective condition.

Also, as general contractor, Defendant failed to designate suitable, competent persons to inspect the premises for safety hazards, such as the improperly covered floor opening.

Also, as general contractor, Defendant failed to assign to a suitable and competent person the task of covering or otherwise guarding the floor opening in a proper manner after Defendant's employees last used the floor opening for access to the basement, prior to the morning of February 24, 1988.

There may be others whose negligence contributed to my injury, to include other contractors on the site during the week prior to February 24, 1988, who had occasion to use the floor opening to the cellar and who may have been directly responsible for not covering the floor opening in a proper manner. Plaintiff's discovery, still unanswered by Defendant, seeks the names of any such other parties as may exist. In any event, as general contractor, Defendant was ultimately responsible for overall safety on this job site, even if the dangerous and defective condition had been directly created by such others.

Q. 19. Please describe the weather at the time of the alleged occurrence and during the 24 hours prior to the alleged occurrence, including whether it was clear, cloudy, raining lightly or sprinkling, raining hard, sleeting, snowing or otherwise, and whether or not there was an accumulation of any type of precipitation around the area of the occurrence.

A. 19. The weather was cold and clear.

Q. 20. Please state fully and in complete detail all that the defendant did or failed to do which in any way caused or contributed to cause the alleged occurrence, including every act or omission of the defendant which you allege constitutes negligence.

A. 20. See answer to Question 18, above, and Question 23, below.

Q. 21. Please identify by name, title, and business address the person with whom you dealt as being the person responsible for, in charge of or supervising the performance of your work on behalf of the owner of the premises at which you were performing your work at the time of the alleged accident.

A. 21. My work was supervised by Mr. Thomas Andrews as president and principal of ACME Construction Company Inc. Mr. Andrews did not supervise the performance of my work as a servant of the owner of the premises but was, on my information, an independent contractor.

Q. 22. If on the day of the alleged accident you were part of a work crew or group, please identify each member of the crew or group by name and residential and business address stating the identity of the person in charge of or in the position as the supervisor of the group and whether any of such persons were present at the time and place of the accident and witnessed the accident.

A. 22. The work crew consisted of the following individuals:

John Williams, 900 Correy Street, Pawtucket, RI.
Karl Amons , 416 Kaspar Lane, Pawtucket, RI.
Thomas Andrews, 40 W. School Rd., Pawtucket, RI,
Supervisor.

Q. 23. If you claim that the defendant in any way
violated any trade standards, safety standards, state,
local or federal governmental regulations in the
production or construction of the dwelling house at
which the accident occurred, please state:

a. the exact standard which it is claimed that the
defendant violated and the respect in which the standard
was violated;

b. how and in what manner this violation caused or
contributed to cause the alleged occurrence.

A. 23. (a) Defendant, as general contractor, violated
the following provisions:

<u>Mass. Division of Industrial Safety</u>
Prevention of Accidents in Construction Operations

411 CMR 10.00 (Effective 1/1/78)
10.03 (1)	Protection of Health & Safety
10.03 (5)	Requirements of Competence
10.03 (7)	Safety Inspections
10.04 (6)	Falling Hazards
(a)	Prevention; and
(b)	Floor Security

Current regulations, 454 CMR 10.00, became effective
on 7/8/88, after Plaintiff's accident, and therefore
Defendant's violations arose under the previous
regulations at 441 CMR 10.00.

<u>OSHA Safety & Health Standards</u>
Construction Industry Standards

29 U.S.C. Part 1926

Subpart C
Sect. 1926.20 Contractor Requirements for Accident
Prevention

Subpart G
Sect. 1926.200(b)   Danger signs
        (c)   Caution signs

Subpart M
Sect. 1926.500 (9) (b) (8), and (f) (5) (ii) Floor hole
guards

        (b)   These violations caused or
contributed to the accident as follows:

<u>Mass. DIS Violations</u>

(1) 441 CMR 10.04 (6) (a) required that every hold or
opening in any floor through which a person may fall
shall have all exposed sides guarded by a barrier
sufficient to prevent falls. This was not done at 10
Maple Drive. If Defendant had complied with this
section, Plaintiff would not have fallen through the
floor opening.

(2) 441 CMR 10.04 (6) (c) required that when floor
openings are covered by solid temporary construction,
such cover shall be properly anchored to prevent
accidental displacement. When ACME left the site a
week before the accident, they had left the floor
opening secured in compliance with this section, by

laying 2x4s across the opening and then nailing plywood onto the 2x4s and through to the decking. This cover was removed when Defendant's employees or others used the floor opening to gain access to the cellar when the concrete floor was poured. This cover was replaced by loose sheets of 1/2 in. plywood laid across the opening, with no timber supports and no nailing, in violation of 10.04 (6) (c). When Plaintiff stepped on the unsecured 1/2 in. plywood, this was not adequate to support his weight, and he fell through the hole. If Defendant had complied with 10.04 (6)(c), the accident would have been prevented.

(3) 441 CMR 10.03 (5) required that the general contractor designate a person of suitable competence to perform in all work. Defendant permitted an incompetent person or persons to perform the task of covering the cellar hole opening after the basement floor was poured.

Also, if Defendant had arranged for daily inspections on the site, Defendant did not designate a person of suitable competence to perform such inspections.

Had a competent person been designated to cover the floor hole after the basement floor was poured, or had a competent person been designated to inspect the site, this accident could have been prevented.

(4) 441 CMR 10.03 (1) (a) required that all work sites be so arranged as to provide reasonable and adequate protection for the safety of employees and others. And 441 CMR 10.03 (1) (b) provided that it is the responsibility of both owners and contractors to provide for such safety. Defendant, both as owner and as general contractor, violated this section by causing or

permitting to exist on the job site a dangerous and defective condition, which consisted of an inadequately constructed floor-hole cover. And this was compounded by Defendant's causing or permitting to exist a plastic sheet which covered and obscured the hazardous condition.

<u>OSHA Violations</u>
29 U.S.C. Part 1926

(1) Subpart C, sect. 1926.20 (b) (1), provides that it is an employer's responsibility to initiate and maintain safety programs on a job site. And sect. 1926.20 (b) (2) provides that this must include frequent and regular inspections. If a competent inspection had been performed at 10 Maple Drive, the accident would have been prevented, where the unsecured and inadequate floor hole cover was a hazard to employees.

(2) Subpart G, Sect. 1926.200 (b) requires that danger signs be posted at dangerous locations on a job site, and Sect. 1926.200 (c) requires that caution signs be posted where potential hazards exist. If, for any valid reason, it was not possible to re-secure the floor hole cover with adequate cross bracing and nailing down, then such danger or hazard should have been signaled by the placement of an appropriate sign. Had such sign been posted, Plaintiff would have been alerted to the fact that the solid floor hole covering had been replaced by an inadequate cover, and this accident could have been prevented. Instead of providing such warning, Defendant caused or permitted to exist a plastic sheet over the floor hole cover, which obscured the hazard.

(3) Subpart M. Sect. 1926.500 (b) (8) provides that floor holes into which a person may fall must be

guarded by either a railing and toe board, or a floor hole cover of standard strength and construction that is secured against accidental displacement. When ACME left the job site a week before the accident, they left the floor hole covered with a secure cover, in compliance with this section. When Plaintiff returned on February 24, 1988, the secure cover had been removed, and it was replaced with one that was of less than standard construction and which was not secured properly. If the floor hole had been properly covered after Defendant's employees or others had worked on the cellar floor, this accident would have been prevented.

Q. 24. Please describe any and all written or oral warnings or instructions given to you in relation to the defect, its existence or use, giving the name and address of each person who gave each such warning or instruction.

A. 24. None.

Subscribed on pain of perjury this 6th day of November, 1990.

_____

Charles Smith

Appendix C Sample Schedule from Subpoena Duces Tecum

SCHEDULE A.

You are requested to bring with you any and all materials of the following descriptions which (a) you referred to in preparing your report of November 28, 1995; and/or (b) to which you may refer in giving testimony at trial.

1. Notes prepared by you in the course of your inspection of the 480DM screener and/or in the course of your research (excluding notes which memorialize communications with counsel or which may otherwise be privileged).

2. Diagrams, blueprints, plans, drawings and sketches.

3. Graphs and/or charts.

4. Records and reports from other persons or entities.

5. Photographs, films and/or videotapes.

6. Deposition excerpts to which you referred in preparing your report.

7. Governmental regulations, including OSHA.

8. Published standards of any industrial or professional associations, including ANSI and ASME.

9.   Non-published written standards from any industrial or professional source.

10.   Product brochures and/or manuals.

11.   Written or transcribed statements of any person.

12.   Treatises and/or publications.

13.   Test results and survey reports.

14.   Physical objects, to include without limitation any exemplar wrenches used by you in performing any test or experiment on the 480DM screener and any instruments used by you in performing any such test or experiment.

Appendix D Sample Notice of Deposition

IN THE COURT OF COMMON PLEAS
WILLIAMS COUNTY, WISCONSIN

STEFAN CARROLL,	)
CASE NO.: 98CV120561	
Plaintiff.	)
	)
JUDGE: SANFORD	
	)
-vs.	)
	)
	)
ACME MOTOR COMPANY,	)
et al.,	)
Defendants	)

NOTICE OF DEPOSITION

Please take notice that on Wednesday, January 13, 1998 at 4:00 pm, plaintiff in the above entitled action will take the deposition pursuant tot he Rules of Civil Procedure, upon oral examination to preserve testimony for trial of:

Wayne Wolfe, Ph.D.

Said deposition will be taken at the offices of Jefferson, Ives, and Associates, 114 Main St., Lakeland, WI   00550 before a court reporter duly authorized to take and transcribe depositions and may be recorded upon videotape pursuant to said rules.

Respectfully submitted,

_____

John M. Jefferson
JEFFERSON, IVES, & Assoc., Co., L.P.A.
114 Main St.
Lakeland, WI   00550
(111) 555-0000

Appendix E Select Rules of Civil Procedure and Evidence

All expert witnesses should familiarize themselves with the Federal Rules of Civil Procedure and Evidence that apply to their testimony. While you will not be arguing points of law with the attorneys, it is helpful to understand the rules that control the litigation. Note that because your state and local rules may vary from the federal rules, you should obtain and compare them with the select federal rules abstracted below.

Federal Rules of Civil Procedure

Rule 26. General Provisions Governing Discovery; Duty of Disclosure

Disclosure of Expert Testimony (2).

(A) In addition to the disclosures required by paragraph (1), a party shall disclose to other parties the identity of any person who may be used at trial to present evidence under Rules 702, 703, or 705 of the Federal Rules of Evidence.

(B) Except as otherwise stipulated or directed by the court, this disclosure shall, with respect to a witness who is retained or specially employed to provide expert testimony in the case or whose duties as an employee of the party regularly involve giving expert testimony, be accompanied by a written report prepared and signed by the witness. The report shall contain a complete statement of all opinions to be expressed and the basis and reasons therefore; the data or other information considered by the witness in forming the opinions; any exhibits to be used as a summary of or support for the opinions; the qualifications of the witness, including a list of all publications authored by the witness within the preceding ten years; the compensation to be paid for the study and testimony; and a listing of any other cases in which the witness has testified as an expert at trial or by deposition within the preceding four years.

(C) These disclosures shall be made at the times and in the sequence directed by the court. In the absence of other directions from the court or stipulation by the parties, the disclosures shall be made at least 90 days before the trial date or the date the case is to be ready for trial or, if the evidence is intended solely to contradict or rebut evidence on the same subject matter identified by another party under paragraph (2)(B), within 30 days after the disclosure made by the other party. The parties shall supplement these disclosures when required under subdivision (e)(1).

The advisory committee notes provide an explanation and interpretation of Rule 26(2)(B) as follows:

Paragraph (2)(B) requires that persons retained or specially employed to provide expert testimony, or whose duties as an employee of the party regularly involve the giving of expert testimony, must prepare a detailed and complete written report, stating the testimony the witness is expected to present during direct examination, together with the reasons therefore. The information disclosed under the former rule in answering interrogatories about the "substance" of expert testimony was frequently so sketchy and vague that it rarely dispensed with the need to depose the expert and often was even of little help in preparing for a deposition of the witness. Revised Rule 37(c)(1) provides an incentive for full disclosure; namely, that a party will not ordinarily be permitted to use on direct examination any expert testimony not so disclosed. Rule 26(a)(2)(B) does not preclude counsel from providing assistance to experts in preparing the reports, and indeed, with experts such as automobile mechanics, this assistance may be needed. Nevertheless, the report, which is intended to set forth the substance of the direct examination, should be written in a manner that reflects the testimony to be given by the witness and it must be signed by the witness.

The report is to disclose the data and other information considered by the expert and any exhibits or charts that summarize or support the expert's opinions. Given this obligation of disclosure, litigants should no longer be able to argue that materials furnished to their experts to be used in forming their opinions — whether or not ultimately relied upon by the expert — are privileged or otherwise protected from disclosure when such persons are testifying or being deposed.

Revised subdivision (b)(4)(A) authorizes the deposition of expert witnesses. Since depositions of experts required to prepare a written report may be taken only after the report has been served, the length of the deposition of such experts should be reduced, and in many cases the report may eliminate the need for a deposition. Revised subdivision (e)(1) requires disclosure of any material changes made in the opinions of an expert from whom a report is required, whether the changes are in the written report or in testimony given at a deposition.

(b)(4) Trial Preparation: Experts.

(A) A party may depose any person who has been identified as an expert whose opinions may be presented at trial. If a report from the expert is required under subdivision (a)(2)(B), the deposition shall not be conducted until after the report is provided.

(B) A party may, through interrogatories or by deposition, discover facts known or opinions held by an expert who has been retained or specially employed by another party in anticipation of litigation or preparation for trial and who is not expected to be called as a witness at trial, only as provided in Rule 35(b) or upon a showing of exceptional circumstances under which it is impracticable for the party seeking discovery to obtain facts or opinions on the same subject by other means.

(C) Unless manifest injustice would result, (i) the court shall require that the party seeking discovery pay the expert a reasonable fee for time spent in responding to discovery under this subdivision; and (ii) with respect to discovery obtained under subdivision (b)(4)(B) of this rule the court shall require the party seeking discovery to pay the other party a fair portion of the fees and expenses reasonable incurred by the latter party in obtaining facts and opinions from the expert.

Federal Rules of Evidence

Rule 601. General Rule of Competency

Every person is competent to be a witness except as otherwise provided in these rules. However, in civil actions and proceedings, with respect to an element of a claim or defense as to which State law supplies the rule of decision, the competency of a witness shall be determined in accordance with State law.

Rule 602. Lack of Personal Knowledge

A witness may not testify to a matter unless evidence is introduced sufficient to support a finding that the witness has personal knowledge of the matter. Evidence to prove personal knowledge may, but need not, consist of the witness' own testimony. This rule is subject to the provisions of rule 703, relating to opinion testimony by the expert witnesses.

Rule 607. Who May Impeach

The credibility of a witness may be attacked by any party, including the party calling the witness.

Rule 608. Evidence of Character and Conduct of Witness

(a) Opinion and reputation evidence of character. The credibility of a witness may be attacked or supported by evidence in the form of opinion or reputation, but subject to these limitations: (1) the evidence may refer only to character for truthfulness or untruthfulness, and (2) evidence of truthful character is admissible only after the character of the witness for truthfulness has been attacked by opinion or reputation evidence or otherwise.

(b) Specific instances of conduct. Specific instances of the conduct of a witness, for the purpose of attacking or supporting the witness' credibility, other than conviction of crime as provided in rule 609, may not be proved by extrinsic evidence. They may, however, in the discretion of the court, if probative of truthfulness or untruthfulness, be inquired into on cross-examination of the witness (1) concerning the witness' character for truthfulness or untruthfulness, or (2) concerning the character for truthfulness or untruthfulness of another witness as to which character the witness being cross-examined has testified.

The giving of testimony, whether by an accused or by any other witness, does not operate as a waiver of the accused's or the witness' privilege against self-incrimination when examined with respect to matters which relate only to credibility.

Rule 609. Impeachment by Evidence of Conviction of Crime

(a) General rule. For the purpose of attacking the credibility of a witness,

(1) evidence that a witness other than an accused has been convicted of a crime shall be admitted, subject to Rule 403, if the crime was punishable by death or imprisonment in excess of one year under the law under which the witness was convicted, and evidence that an accused has been convicted of such a crime shall be admitted if the court determines that the probative value of admitting this evidence outweighs its prejudicial effect to the accused; and

(2) evidence that any witness has been convicted of a crime shall be admitted if it involved dishonesty or false statement, regardless of the punishment.

(b) Time limit. Evidence of a conviction under this rule is not admissible if a period of more than ten years has elapsed since the date of the conviction or of the release of the witness from the confinement imposed for that conviction, whichever is the later date, unless the court determines, in the interests of justice, that the probative value of the conviction supported by specific facts and circumstances substantially outweighs its prejudicial effect. However, evidence of a conviction more than 10 years old as calculated herein, is not admissible unless the proponent gives to the adverse party sufficient advance written notice of intent to use such evidence to provide the adverse party with a fair opportunity to contest the use of such evidence.

(c) Effect of pardon, annulment, or certificate of rehabilitation. Evidence of a conviction is not admissible under this rule if (1) the conviction has been the subject of a pardon, annulment, certificate of rehabilitation, or other equivalent procedure based on a finding of the rehabilitation of the person convicted, and that person has not been convicted of a subsequent crime which was punishable by death or imprisonment in excess of one year, or (2) the conviction has been the subject of a pardon, annulment, or other equivalent procedure based on a finding of innocence.

(d) Juvenile adjudications. Evidence of juvenile adjudications is generally not admissible under this rule. The court may, however, in a criminal case allow evidence of a juvenile adjudication of a witness other than the accused if conviction of the offense would be admissible to attack the credibility of an adult and the court is satisfied that admission in evidence is necessary for a fair determination of the issue of guilt or innocence.

(e) Pendency of appeal. The pendency of an appeal therefrom does not render evidence of a conviction inadmissible. Evidence of the pendency of an appeal is admissible.

Rule 611. Mode and Order of Interrogation and Presentation

(a) Control by court. The court shall exercise reasonable control over the mode and order of interrogating witnesses and presenting evidence so as to (1) make the interrogation and presentation effective for the ascertainment of the truth, (2) avoid needless consumption of time, and (3) protect witnesses from harassment or undue embarrassment.

(b) Scope of cross-examination. Cross-examination should be limited to the subject matter of the direct examination and matters affecting the credibility of the witness. The court may, in the exercise of discretion, permit inquiry into additional matters as if on direct examination.

(c) Leading questions. Leading questions should not be used on the direct examination of a witness except as may be necessary to develop the witness' testimony. Ordinarily leading questions should be permitted on cross-examination. When a party calls a hostile witness, an adverse party, or a witness identified with an adverse party, interrogation may be by leading question.

Rule 613. Prior Statements of Witnesses

(a) Examining witness concerning prior statement. In examining a witness concerning a prior statement made by the witness, whether written or not, the statement need not be shown nor its contents disclosed to the witness at that time, but on request the same shall be shown or disclosed to opposing counsel.

(b) Extrinsic evidence of prior inconsistent statement of witness. Extrinsic evidence of a prior inconsistent statement by a witness is not admissible unless the witness is afforded an opportunity to explain or deny the same and the opposite party is afforded an opportunity to interrogate the witness thereon, or the interests of justice otherwise require. This provision does not apply to admissions of a party-opponent as defined in rule 801(d)(2).

Rule 701. Opinion Testimony by Lay Witnesses

If the witness is not testifying as an expert, the witness' testimony in the form of opinions or inferences is limited to those opinions or inferences which are (a) rationally based on the perception of the witness and (b) helpful to a clear understanding of the witness' testimony or the determination of a fact in issue.

Rule 702. Testimony by Experts

If scientific, technical, or other specialized knowledge will assist the trier of fact to understand the evidence or to determine a fact in issue, a witness qualified as an expert by knowledge, skill, experience, training, or education, may testify thereto in the form of an opinion or otherwise.

Rule 703. Bases of Opinion Testimony by Experts

The facts or data in the particular case upon which an expert bases an opinion may be those perceived by or made known to the expert at or before the hearing. If of a type reasonably relied upon by experts in the particular field in forming opinions or inferences upon the subject, the facts or data need not be admissible in evidence.

Rule 704. Opinion on Ultimate Issue

(a) Except as provided in subdivision (b), testimony in the form of an opinion or inference otherwise admissible is not objectionable because it embraces an ultimate issue to be decided by the trier of fact.

(b) No expert witness testifying with respect to the mental state or condition of a defendant in a criminal case may state an opinion or inference as to whether the defendant did or did not have the mental state or condition constituting an element of the crime charged or of a defense thereto. Such ultimate issues are matters for the trier of fact alone.

Rule 705. Disclosure of Facts or Data Underlying Expert Opinion

The expert may testify in terms of opinion or inference and give reasons therefor without first testifying to the underlying facts or data, unless the court requires otherwise. The expert may in any event be required to disclose the underlying facts or data on cross-examination.

Rule 706. Court Appointed Experts

(a) Appointment. The court may on its own motion or on the motion of any party enter an order to show cause why expert witnesses should not be appointed, and may request the parties to submit nominations. The court may appoint any expert witnesses agreed upon by the parties, and may appoint expert witnesses of its own selection. An expert witness shall not be appointed by the court unless the witness consents to act. A witness so appointed shall be informed of the witness' duties by the court in writing, a copy of which shall be filed with the clerk, or at a conference in which the parties shall have opportunity to participate. A witness so appointed shall advise the parties of the witness' findings, if any; the witness' deposition may be taken by any party; and the witness may be called to testify by the court or any party. The witness shall be subject to cross-examination by each party, including a party calling the witness.

(b) Compensation. Expert witnesses so appointed are entitled to reasonable compensation in whatever sum the court may allow. The compensation thus fixed is payable from funds which may be provided by law in criminal cases and civil actions and proceedings involving just compensation under the fifth amendment. In other civil actions and proceedings the compensation shall be paid by the parties in such proportion and at such time as the court directs, and thereafter charged in like manner as other costs.

(c) Disclosure of appointment. In the exercise of its discretion, the court may authorize disclosure to the jury of the fact that the court appointed the expert witness.

(d) Parties' experts of own selection. Nothing in this rule limits the parties in calling expert witnesses of their own selection.

Rule 1005. Public Records

The contents of an official record, or of a document authorized to be recorded or filed and actually recorded or filed, including data compilations in any form, if otherwise admissible, may be proved by copy, certified as correct in accordance with rule 902 or testified to be correct by a witness who has compared it with the original. If a copy which complies with the foregoing cannot be obtained by the exercise of reasonable diligence, then other evidence of the contents may be given.

Rule 1006. Summaries

The contents of voluminous writings, recordings, or photographs which cannot conveniently be examined in court may be presented in the form of a chart, summary, or calculation. The originals, or duplicates, shall be made available for examination or copying, or both, by other parties at reasonable time and place. The court may order that they be produced in court.

Rule 1007. Testimony or Written Admission of Party

Contents of writings, recordings, or photographs may be proved by the testimony or deposition of the party against whom offered or by that party's written admission, without accounting for the nonproduction of the original.

Index

gathering, 27-28, 89
unwanted disclosure of, 145-146
Injury, workplace, 2, 82-83, 103-108, 115, 116, 120-122, 166-167,
169-173, 177, 178, 189-190
Instructions not to answer, 15-16
Intellectual rigor, 102-103
Interrogatories, 4, 7, 39, 92-95, 233-257
Interrogatory answers, 92-95
Interruptions, 145
to questions and answers, 152
Intimidation, 30-32

Jokes, 22-23, 164
Jury, 19, 22-24, 27-28, 30, 32, 46, 63, 64, 68, 71, 75, 76, 77, 79,
90, 92, 111, 114, 120, 122, 126, 130, 137, 138, 139, 148, 149,
153, 154, 155, 157, 158, 159, 162-163, 164, 166, 167, 177,
178, 187, 189, 209, 210, 215, 216, 217, 222
Jury instructions, 39
Justifying your fee, 206-207

Laboratory values, 22, 34
Lawyer tactics, 71, 84, 122, 128, 130, 157, 183, 196-197, 198, 213,
221, 224
Lawyers, disputes between, 13, 64, 65-66, 95, 154-155, 221
Leading questions, 10, 177, 190
Learning about the opponent's case, 32-36
Legal standards, 39, 40, 189
Liability, legal standards for, 39
Limits to discovery, 5-9
Listening carefully, 13, 15, 135, 152-153, 155, 165-166
Litigation, status of, 39, 40
Live testimony, 3, 17, 116, 209, 212
Local and state rules, 3, 10, 64, 156, 205, 263
Locking in testimony, 18, 20-22, 71, 92
Looking good for the camera, 212-213

M.T. McBrian, Inc. v. Liebert Corp., 206
Magic words, 40
Malpractice, 51, 52
Marking exhibits, 58
Materiality, 12
Memorization, 45, 153-154
Methodology, 18, 71, 81, 100-108, 230

for opinions, 86-87, 230
Reading and signing the deposition, 9-11, 156-157, 184, 205, 206, 231
Reasonable degree of certainty, 40, 82, 151, 185, 189
Reasonable fee, 201-202, 204, 205, 206
Record,
    discussions off the, 3, 155
    discussions on the, 3, 152, 202, 207, 223, 224
Records, availability of, 144, 147
Red-herring, 122
Redirecting counsel, 34
Relevancy, 10, 12, 106-108
Reliability, 101-103, 106-108, 187
Repetitive questioning, 220, 221-222, 226
Reports,
    knowing your own, 48-49, 95, 230
    when received, 45, 230
Reputation, 47, 53, 64
Requests for admissions, 4
Rescheduling the deposition, 50, 52, 207
Rules and procedures, 210-212
Run-through, 39

Sanctions, 8-9, 66, 220, 224
Sanitizing files, 63
Sarcasm, 164, 223-225
Schedule, 53, 54, 55, 259-260
Scheduling conflicts, 50, 51-52
Scientific standards, 101, 106-108, 144
Settlement of case, 4, 18, 19, 22, 32, 36, 71, 86, 157
Sheehan v. Daily Racing Form, Inc., 102
Signing the deposition, 9-11, 156-157, 184, 205, 206, 231
Silence, of counsel, 157
Slang, avoid, 182-183
Softballs, 82, 83
Soundbite questions, 112
Speaking objections, 13-15
Speculation, 151-152, 166, 185, 188-189
Staff, 144, 146
Standard stipulations, 9-11
Stasior v. National Railroad Passenger Corp., 103, 108
State and local rules, 3, 10, 156, 205, 263
Status of litigation, 39, 40